UK Tower Air Fryer Cookbook 2024

1800 Days of Quick, Healthy and Delicious Recipes Using UK Measurements & Ingredients for Your Whole Family and Busy People on a Budget (FULL COLOUR EDITION)

James Hoyle

Copyright © 2023 By James Hoyle All rights reserved.

No part of this book may be reproduced, transmitted, or distributed in any form or by any means without permission in writing from the publisher except in the case of brief quotations embodied in critical articles or reviews.

Legal & Disclaimer

The content and information in this book is consistent and truthful, and it has been provided for informational, educational and business purposes only.

The illustrations in the book are from the website shutterstock.com, depositphoto.com and freepik.com and have been authorized.

The content and information contained in this book has been compiled from reliable sources, which are accurate based on the knowledge, belief, expertise and information of the Author. The author cannot be held liable for any omissions and/or errors.

TABLE OF CONTENT

INTRODUCTION	**01**
CHAPTER 1: UNDERSTANDING THE TOWER AIR FRYER	**02**
CHAPTER 2: BREAKFAST AND BRUNCH RECIPES	**08**
CHAPTER 3: VEGETARIAN AND VEGETABLE RECIPES	**17**
CHAPTER 4: POULTRY RECIPES	**26**
CHAPTER 5: FISH AND SEAFOOD RECIPES	**36**
CHAPTER 6: BEEF, LAMB AND PORK RECIPES	**45**
CHAPTER 7: SNACKS RECIPES	**54**
CHAPTER 8: DESSERT RECIPES	**62**
APPENDIX 1: MEASUREMENT CONVERSION CHART	**70**
APPENDIX 2: RECIPES INDEX	**71**

INTRODUCTION

Having the best cutting-edge air frying technology, Tower's convenient air fryer can fry, roast, dehydrate, or bake with little to no oil. Tower has introduced the efficient Vortx Technology into its air fryers which lets you enjoy the flavour of deep-fried food with only 10% of the fat content. Using the hot, moving air convection, this air fryer quickly cooks food that is crispy on the outside and moist inside. I have recently had the experience of introducing the Tower Air Fryer into my kitchen and it has made quick and convenient cooking possible for me. To test this appliance I tried all sorts of recipes and each time this appliance surprised me more than before.

This Tower Air Fryer Recipe Cookbook is for all the cooking enthusiasts who enjoy cooking delicious and healthy meals at home. If you have Tower air frying technology at home, then the complete collection of over 120 air fryer recipes in this cookbook will help you create an amazing menu for your dinner table. Using my over 120 recipes you can cook delicious breakfasts, entrees, desserts, and crispy snacks for routine meals and for all sorts of festivities.

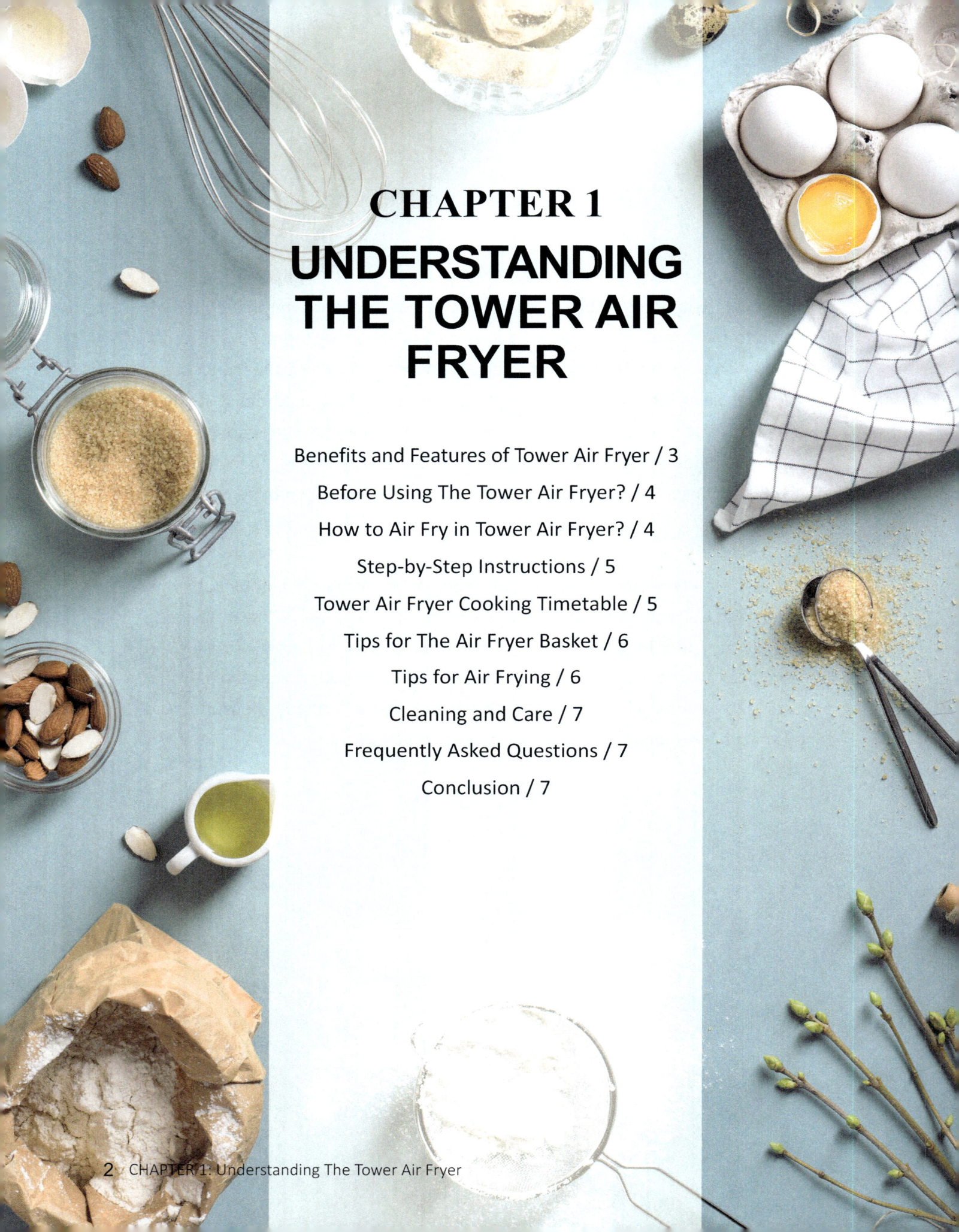

CHAPTER 1
UNDERSTANDING THE TOWER AIR FRYER

Benefits and Features of Tower Air Fryer / 3

Before Using The Tower Air Fryer? / 4

How to Air Fry in Tower Air Fryer? / 4

Step-by-Step Instructions / 5

Tower Air Fryer Cooking Timetable / 5

Tips for The Air Fryer Basket / 6

Tips for Air Frying / 6

Cleaning and Care / 7

Frequently Asked Questions / 7

Conclusion / 7

Tower promises to satisfy all of your air frying demands and has the widest selection of air fryers in the UK. As only the Tower Air Fryer has Vortx Technology, you can make meals that are almost entirely fat-free in addition to cooking 30% faster than other air fryers. Try one of the air fryers now, and you'll start to wonder how you ever got along without one! The great thing about Tower Air Fryers is that due to their efficiency, they help you save so much on your electricity bill. They are not only fast and quick but they are also small and compact in size which makes them portable, and perfect for small kitchen spaces. You can keep these air fryers in your hostel dorm, in your RV and in hotel rooms. It is designed with a versatile control panel to provide you multiple cooking options like air fry, dehydrate, roast, or bake.

Benefits and Features of Tower Air Fryer

Every electric cooking appliance is a blessing for all homemakers as well as people with an ever-busy lifestyle. These devices bring great convenience and ease to the process of cooking. Besides these obvious benefits of this cooking appliance, the Tower Air Fryer offers so many other great advantages due to its supreme quality, versatile functions and stable built and size. From its size to its cooking functions, this Air fryer can serve the best to cook crispy and crunchy food in no time. Let's see what more it can offer you in the kitchen.

Healthy Cooking
Air frying as a cooking method is healthy. It roasts or cooks the food using nothing but hot air. It gives the food the same crispy texture as deep frying but stops you from the use of heavy oils or fats. By using a spray of cooking oil, you can cook any amount of food in this Air fryer. Its heating system is installed in such a position that food is cooked in a closed pressurized vessel which further makes the air frying more effective. Further, the closed vessel cooking technology keeps the food protected from any form of contamination, as long as you are not ready to serve the meal, the food can be kept safe and stored in the Air fryer basket. The ceramic coating in its basket does not release any chemicals or harmful agents into the food which also makes this device health effective.

Fast and Efficient Technology
The same food that takes hours of cooking on the stovetop can be cooked in a few minutes using the Tower Air Fryer. Its smart and efficient heating mechanism provides even heat to the food from all sides which allow quick cooking. Moreover, the heat is effectively retained inside the vessel without any loss to the environment which makes it more efficient in cooking. When the hot air is passed through the food, it instantly cooks the food. Using high-temperature settings you can cook any food in no time.

Good for Small Space
The Tower Air Fryer is more like a cylindrical vessel with a broad base. So in spite of providing sufficient space for the food to cook, it takes up considerably small space in your kitchen. It can be kept on any kitchen shelf or working place. It has a firm and strong build with a stable structure, so it is easy to keep at any place in the kitchen. It is also easy to handle and can be moved easily, so you can clean the space below and around it.

User-Friendly Control Panel

By looking at the control panel of the Tower Air Fryer, you will realize how simple and user-friendly its mechanism is. You don't need to constantly check and set the hardware or the software. Just plug it in and select the desired mode, time and temperature, and press start. By its single-button technology, it gives easier access to all of its users. The preset modes allow even easier handling of the device. The assembly of all of its accessories from the air fryer basket to the crisper plate and the rack is also quite simple. Follow the steps discussed above, and anyone can become a Tower Air Fryer expert. It takes just 2 to 3 sessions of cooking with the device to fully understand its control.

Before Using The Tower Air Fryer?

Due to its distinctive size, shape, and appearance, every model of the Tower Air Fryer is easy to identify. Unlike multipurpose cookers, this air fryer uses a straightforward cooking technique. The complete apparatus consists of a base that houses the heating system and has room for the food basket to be inserted. This user-friendly approach makes the Air Fryer extremely clever and practical for all of its customers. Simply adding food to the basket and placing it bake into the air fryer, is all that is required. Choose the proper timing and temperature for cooking the food, and the appliance will take care of the rest.

Test Run

Before utilizing the air fryer for cooking, you should test it at least once. This will help you in becoming familiar with the various features of your air fryer and ensure that it is operating properly. The air fryer can be examined as follows:

Connect the air fryer's power plug. A full air fryer basket should be used. Next, give the air fryer some time to warm up. You will see a preheat button on your air fryer if it has multiple functions. Small, pricey air fryers typically use analogue control systems. These will need to be manually warmed up. Manually preheat the Tower Air Fryer for 5 minutes at 200 °C. When the preheating process is finished, the air fryer will beep. After that, remove the air fryer's basket and give it five minutes to cool. After that, return the empty basket inside the air fryer.

How to Air Fry in Tower Air Fryer?

Prior to using the air fryer for cooking, it must be preheated. This is so that the food will cook more quickly and have a crispy exterior when the air fryer is preheated. By pushing the preheat button, you can quickly pre-heat a multi-function device. However, you will need to manually preheat small, inexpensive air fryers. For manual preheating, turn the air fryer on for 5 minutes at 200 °C.

Automatic Switch Off:

A built-in timer on the Tower Air Fryer will turn the appliance off when the countdown approaches zero. The timer dial can be manually turned off by rotating it counterclockwise to 0.

Drawer Safety Switch for an Air Fryer:

This air fryer has a safety switch in the drawer for your protection to prevent it from unintentionally turning on when the timer is not set and the frying basket and drawer are not correctly positioned within the appliance. Please make sure the drawer is completely closed, the basket is inserted correctly, and the cooking time is set before using the air fryer.

4 CHAPTER 1: Understanding The Tower Air Fryer

Step-by-Step Instructions

The power plug should be plugged into an earthed wall outlet. Remove the drawer from the air fryer with care. Fill the basket with the ingredients. Making sure to properly align it with the guides in the fryer's body, slide the drawer back into the air fryer. Use the drawer only with the basket inside. Avoid touching the drawer right away after using it since it gets quite hot. Give it plenty of time to cool. Hold the drawer solely by the handle. Determine the amount of time your ingredients need to be prepared. Set the timer dial to the amount of time needed to prepare the appliance before turning it on.

Set the temperature control dial to what is needed. When the appliance is cold, the preparation time is increased by 3 minutes. If you choose, you can also pre-heat (but not cook) the gadget without any food inside. In order to accomplish this, set the timer dial to a duration greater than 3 minutes, then wait until the heating-up light disappears (after approximately 3 minutes). Fill the basket once the light goes out, then set the timer dial to the amount of time needed for preparation.

The timer will start to count down from the designated preparation time. The working light will intermittently turn on and off when the food is being fried in hot air. In order to keep the desired temperature, the heating element is turned on and off. Extra oil from the ingredients settles into the drawer's bottom. Halfway through the preparation period, some ingredients must be shaken. Pull the drawer out of the air fryer appliance by the handle, then shake the ingredients in it. Then lower the drawer into the fryer once more. Precaution: Avoid pressing the handle's basket release button while shaking.

As a weight-reducing method, you can take the basket out of the drawer and shake it separately. Pull the drawer from the appliance, set it on a heat-resistant surface, press the handle button, and then lift the basket out of the drawer to accomplish this. When it's time to shake the ingredients, the timer bell will ring if you set it to half the preparation time. The timer will then need to be reset to the amount of preparation time left.

Once the time allotted for set preparation passes you hear the timer ring. Place the drawer in a suitable work area after removing it from the device. You can also manually turn the appliance off. Turn the timer control dial to 0 to accomplish this. Verify that the ingredients are prepared. Simply re-insert the drawer into the air fryer and increase the timer's setting if the ingredients aren't quite ready.

Pull the drawer from the air fryer and set it down on a suitable surface before pressing the basket release button and lifting the basket out of the drawer to remove contents (such as fries). Avoid inverting the basket while the drawer is still attached because any extra oil that has accumulated on the drawer's bottom will drip onto the ingredients. The ingredients and the drawer will both be extremely hot. Care must be taken since steam may escape from the drawer depending on the sort of items in the fryer. Put the contents of the basket in a bowl or on a plate. Use a pair of tongs to pull heavy or delicate things out of the basket.

Tower Air Fryer Cooking Timetable

FOOD TYPE	MIN-MAX(G)	TEMP(°C)	TIME (MIN)	SHAKE	REMARK
Potato and Fries					
Thin Frozen Fries	400-500	200	18-20	Shake	
Thick Frozen Fries	400-500	200	20-25	Shake	
Potato Gratin	600	200	20-25	Shake	

CHAPTER 1: Understanding The Tower Air Fryer

FOOD TYPE	MIN-MAX(G)	TEMP(°C)	TIME (MIN)	SHAKE	REMARK
Meat and Poultry					
Steak	100-600	180	10-15		Remark
Pork Chops	100-600	180	10-15		
Hamburger	100-600	180	10-15		
Sausage Roll	100-600	200	13-15		
Drumsticks	100-600	180	25-30		
Chicken Breast	100-600	180	15-20		
Snacks					
Spring Rolls	100-500	200	8-10	Shake	Use Oven-Ready
Frozen Chicken Nuggets	100-600	200	6-10	Shake	Use Oven-Ready
Frozen Fish Finger	100-500	200	6-10		Use Oven-Ready
Frozen Bread Crumbed Cheese Snack	100-500	180	8-10		Use Oven-Ready
Stuffed Vegetables	100-500	160	10		
Snacks					
Cake	400	160	20-25		Use Baking Tin
Quiche	500	180	20-22		Use Baking Tin or Oven Dish
Muffins	400	200	15-18		Use Baking Tin
Sweet Snacks	500	160	20		Use Baking Tin or Oven Dish

Tips for The Air Fryer Basket

Only remove the air fryer's basket when cooking and cleaning food. Avoid repeatedly removing the basket. The handle's button guard stops the user from unintentionally hitting the release button. To release the basket, slide the button guard forward. When taking out the basket, never hit the basket release button. This is because the basket may fall and create mishaps if the release button is pressed while the basket is being carried. When you're ready, merely press the basket release button. Make sure the surface you plan to set it on is secure and heat-resistant. The air fryer's handle is affixed to the inside basket rather than the outside basket. As a result, your outer basket will drop when you press the release button on the basket.

Tips for Air Frying

Your ingredient sizes will determine how long it takes to prepare. Smaller portions might cook more quickly.

- Smaller ingredients should be stirred halfway through the cooking process to enhance the outcome and to avoid unevenly fried items.
- To make raw potatoes crispy, add some oil to them. Within a few minutes of adding the oil to the air fryer, begin frying your ingredients.
- Use extreme caution when air-frying foods that are incredibly oily, such as sausages.
- The air fryer can be used to produce snacks that can be made in an oven.
- 300 grams is the ideal weight for making crispy fries.
- To quickly and conveniently produce filled snacks, use the pre-made dough. Additionally, the prepared dough needs less time to prepare than homemade dough.
- If you wish to bake a delicious cake or quiche or if you want to fry delicate ingredients or filler ingredients, place a baking pan or oven dish in the air fryer basket.
- The Tower Air Fryer can also be used to reheat food. Set the fryer to 150°C and leave it there for up to 10 minutes to warm the ingredients.

Cleaning and Care

The appliance should not be submerged in water or any other liquid. Each time you use the appliance, clean it. To avoid damaging the non-stick coating, avoid using metal kitchen tools or abrasive cleaning supplies to clean the drawer or basket. After removing the mains plug from the outlet, wait for the appliance to cool. Removing the drawer will let the air fryer cool down more quickly. Utilize a wet towel to clean the appliance's outside.

With hot water, some dishwashing solutions, and a non-abrasive sponge, clean the drawer and basket. To get rid of any leftover dirt, apply degreasing fluid. The drawer and basket should only be washed by hand. any component of this appliance should not be put in the dishwasher.

Fill the drawer with hot water and little dishwashing solutions to remove dirt that has adhered to the bottom of the drawer or the basket. The drawer and the basket should soak for about 10 minutes after being placed in the drawer. Utilizing a non-abrasive sponge and hot water, clean the interior of the appliance. To get rid of any food stains, clean the heating element using a cleaning brush. Before storing the appliance, make sure it is cool, tidy, and dry. Keep the appliance in a cool, dry location.

Frequently Asked Questions

1. How long should the Tower Air Fryer cool completely before being stored?
Before storing or cleaning, I advise letting the Tower Air Fryer 30 to 45 minutes cool.

2. I need to make my homemade fries more crispy. What ought I do?
Before adding oil to the fries and placing them in the Air Fryer, make sure they are absolutely dry. For a crispier outcome, try chopping the potatoes into smaller, thinner fries and adding a little bit of extra oil.

3. What to do if the basket won't fit in its position properly?
You might have stuffed the basket with too many ingredients. Make sure you don't overfill the basket; the maximum load line should be followed.

4. How much cooking oil should I use for cooking in the Tower Air Fryer?
No additional oil is needed for partially frozen fried items. For other meals, merely add 1/2 to 1 tbsp of oil.

5. The Air Fryer is emitting white smoke. What should I do?
If you are cooking with oily items, a lot of oil will flow into the drawer, which is typical. This has no impact on the device or the outcome.

6. Is shaking food necessary during cooking?
For even cooking and good results, the food should be tossed in the basket. For that do not shake the entire unit, but pause the cooking operation first then remove the basket from the fryer. Shake the food or toss or flip it then resume the cooking process. Though this step is not necessary in all cases. But it is often recommended when you are using the Tower Air Fryer.

Conclusion

Smart Air frying has now become easier than ever, all thanks to the Tower's multipurpose and efficient Air Fryer. All chefs and homemakers can enjoy cooking with this appliance, as it allows us to quickly cook crispy foods, whether it's fried chicken, meat, seafood or vegetables all in one pot. You can get consistently good results in this sleek-looking Tower Air Fryer. With over 120 Tower Air Fryer recipes, you can cook all your favourite breakfasts, lunch, and meals at home. Not only that, but this recipe collection is also bringing you the best of the best snacks and dessert ideas to cook in your air fryer. So, go ahead! Do give these recipes a try and create a wholesome menu for your dinner table.

CHAPTER 1: Understanding The Tower Air Fryer

CHAPTER 2
BREAKFAST AND BRUNCH RECIPES

Air Fryer Sausage / 9

Breakfast Courgette and Pepper / 9

Cheese Broccoli Quiche / 10

Cheesy Courgette Fritters / 10

Chicken and Broccoli Quiche / 11

Cinnamon French Toast Sticks / 11

Egg Mushroom Frittata / 12

Feta Sausage Frittata / 12

Spicy Sausage Streaky Rasher Fandango / 13

Toad-in-the-Hole Tarts / 13

Breakfast Sausage and Potato Bake / 14

Creamy Chilli Soufflé / 14

Cheesy Pak Choi and Egg Frittata / 14

Eggs, Tomato and Mushrooms Scramble / 15

Garlic Tofu and Mushroom Omelette / 15

Sausage Solo / 15

Cheddar Breakfast Pockets / 16

Tex-Mex Hash Browns / 16

Air Fryer Sausage

⏱ PREP TIME: 5 MINUTES, COOK TIME: 20 MINUTES, SERVES 5

🍷 INGREDIENTS
- 5 raw and uncooked sausage links

What you'll need from the store cupboard:
- 15 ml olive oil

🍳 DIRECTIONS
1. Preheat the Air fryer to 180 ºC and grease the Air fryer basket with olive oil.
2. Flip the sausages in the basket and air fry for about 15 minutes.
3. Cook for 5 more minutes and serve warm.

Nutrition Facts Per Serving:
Calories: 131, Fat: 11.8g, Carbohydrates: 0g, Sugar: 0g, Protein: 6g, Sodium: 160mg

---

Breakfast Courgette and Pepper

⏱ PREP TIME: 5 MINUTES, COOK TIME: 25 MINUTES, SERVES 4

🍷 INGREDIENTS
- 4 courgettes, diced into 2-cm pieces, drained
- 2 small bell pepper, chopped medium
- 2 small onion, chopped medium

What you'll need from the store cupboard:
- Cooking oil spray
- Pinch salt and black pepper

🍳 DIRECTIONS
1. Preheat the Air fryer to 175 ºC and grease the Air fryer basket with cooking spray.
2. Season the courgette with salt and black pepper and place in the Air fryer basket.
3. Select Roasting mode and air fry for about 20 minutes, stirring occasionally.
4. Add onion and bell pepper and air fry for 5 more minutes.
5. Remove from the Air fryer and mix well to serve warm.

Nutrition Facts Per Serving:
Calories: 146, Fat: 0.5g, Carbohydrates: 3.8g, Sugar: 5.5g, Protein: 4g, Sodium: 203mg

CHAPTER 2: Breakfast and Brunch Recipes

Cheese Broccoli Quiche

⏱ PREP TIME: 10 MINUTES, COOK TIME: 40 MINUTES, SERVES 2

INGREDIENTS
- 1 large broccoli, chopped into florets
- 3 large carrots, peeled and diced
- 115 g cheddar cheese, grated
- 30 g feta cheese
- 2 large eggs

What you'll need from the store cupboard:
- 1 tsp. dried rosemary
- 1 tsp. dried thyme
- Salt and black pepper, to taste

DIRECTIONS
1. Preheat the Air fryer to 180 ºC and grease a quiche dish.
2. Place broccoli and carrots into a food steamer and air fry for about 20 minutes until soft.
3. Whisk together eggs with dried herbs, salt and black pepper in a bowl.
4. Place steamed vegetables at the bottom of the quiche pan and top with cheddar and feta cheese.
5. Drizzle with the egg mixture and transfer the quiche dish in the Air fryer.
6. Bake for about 20 minutes and dish out to serve warm.

Nutrition Facts Per Serving:
Calories: 412, Fat: 28g, Carbohydrates: 16.3g, Sugar: 7.5g, Protein: 25.3g, Sodium: 720mg

---

Cheesy Courgette Fritters

⏱ PREP TIME: 15 MINUTES, COOK TIME: 7 MINUTES, SERVES 4

INGREDIENTS
- 300 g courgette, grated and squeezed
- 200 g Halloumi cheese
- 35 g plain flour
- 2 eggs
- 1 tsp. fresh dill, minced

What you'll need from the store cupboard:
- Salt and black pepper, to taste

DIRECTIONS
1. Preheat the Air fryer to 180 ºC and grease a baking dish.
2. Mix together all the ingredients in a large bowl.
3. Make small fritters from this mixture and place them on the prepared baking dish.
4. Transfer the dish in the Air Fryer basket and bake for about 7 minutes.
5. Dish out and serve warm.

Nutrition Facts Per Serving:
Calories: 250, Fat: 17.2g, Carbohydrates: 10g, Sugar: 2.7g, Protein: 15.2g, Sodium: 330mg

CHAPTER 2: Breakfast and Brunch Recipes

Chicken and Broccoli Quiche

⏱ PREP TIME: 15 MINUTES, COOK TIME: 12 MINUTES, SERVES 4

🏆 INGREDIENTS

- 1 frozen ready-made shortcrust pastry
- 1 egg
- 30 g cheddar cheese, grated
- 18 g boiled broccoli, chopped
- 50 g cooked chicken, chopped

What you'll need from the store cupboard:

- ½ tbsp. olive oil
- 45 ml double cream
- Salt and black pepper, to taste

🍳 DIRECTIONS

1. Preheat the Air fryer to 200 °C and grease 2 small pie dishes with olive oil.
2. Whisk egg with double cream, cheese, salt and black pepper in a bowl.
3. Cut 2 (13-cm) rounds from the shortcrust pastry and arrange in each pie dish.
4. Press in the bottom and sides gently and pour the egg mixture over pie crust.
5. Top evenly with chicken and broccoli and place the pie dishes into an Air Fryer basket.
6. Bake for about 12 minutes and dish out to serve hot.

Nutrition Facts Per Serving:
Calories: 166, Fat: 10.3g, Carbohydrates: 14.6g, Sugar: 8.5g, Protein: 4.2g, Sodium: 186mg

---

Cinnamon French Toast Sticks

⏱ PREP TIME: 10 MINUTES, COOK TIME: 5 MINUTES, SERVES 4

🏆 INGREDIENTS

- 4 bread, sliced into sticks
- 30 g soft butter or margarine
- 2 eggs, gently beaten
- Salt, to taste
- 1 pinch cinnamon
- 1 pinch nutmeg
- 1 pinch ground cloves

What you'll need from the store cupboard:

🍳 DIRECTIONS

1. Preheat the Air fryer at 185 °C and grease an Air fryer pan with butter.
2. Whisk eggs with salt, cinnamon, nutmeg and ground cloves in a bowl.
3. Dip the bread sticks in the egg mixture and place in the pan.
4. Bake for about 5 minutes, flipping in between and remove from the Air fryer.
5. Dish out and serve warm.

Nutrition Facts Per Serving:
Calories: 186, Fat: 11.7g, Carbohydrates: 6.8g, Sugar: 1.7g, Protein: 13.2g, Sodium: 498mg

CHAPTER 2: Breakfast and Brunch Recipes

Egg Mushroom Frittata

PREP TIME: 10 MINUTES, COOK TIME: 18 MINUTES, SERVES 2

INGREDIENTS

- 4 eggs
- 120 ml milk
- 2 green onions, chopped
- 20 g baby Bella mushrooms, chopped
- 15 g spinach, chopped

What you'll need from the store cupboard:
- 15 g butter
- ½ tsp. salt
- ½ tsp. black pepper
- Dash of hot sauce

DIRECTIONS

1. Preheat the Air fryer to 185 ºC and grease 15x7.5 cm square pan with butter.
2. Whisk eggs with milk in a large bowl and stir in green onions, mushrooms and spinach.
3. Sprinkle with salt, black pepper and hot sauce and pour this mixture into the prepared pan.
4. Place in the Air fryer and bake for about 18 minutes.
5. Dish out in a platter and serve warm.

Nutrition Facts Per Serving:
Calories: 166, Fat: 10.1g, Carbohydrates: 5.8g, Sugar: 4g, Protein: 13.8g, Sodium: 748mg

Feta Sausage Frittata

PREP TIME: 15 MINUTES, COOK TIME: 11 MINUTES, SERVES 2

INGREDIENTS

- ½ of chorizo sausage, sliced
- 85 g frozen corn
- 1 large potato, boiled, peeled and cubed
- 3 jumbo eggs
- 30 g feta cheese, crumbled

What you'll need from the store cupboard:
- 15 ml olive oil
- Salt and black pepper, to taste

DIRECTIONS

1. Preheat the Air fryer to 180 ºC and grease an Air Fryer pan.
2. Whisk together eggs with salt and black pepper in a bowl.
3. Heat olive oil in the Air Fryer pan and add sausage, corn and potato.
4. Air fry for about 6 minutes and stir in the whisked eggs.
5. Top with cheese and bake for about 5 minutes.
6. Dish out and serve hot.

Nutrition Facts Per Serving:
Calories: 327, Fat: 20.2g, Carbohydrates: 23.3g, Sugar: 2.8g, Protein: 15.3g, Sodium: 316mg

Spicy Sausage Streaky Rasher Fandango

PREP TIME: 5 MINUTES, COOK TIME: 20 MINUTES, SERVES 4

INGREDIENTS
- 8 streaky rashers
- 8 chicken sausages
- 4 eggs

What you'll need from the store cupboard:
- Salt and black pepper, to taste

DIRECTIONS
1. Preheat the Air fryer to 160 ºC and grease 4 ramekins lightly.
2. Place streaky rashers and sausages in the Air fryer basket.
3. Air fry for about 10 minutes and crack 1 egg in each prepared ramekin.
4. Season with salt and black pepper and cook for about 10 more minutes.
5. Divide streaky rashers and sausages in serving plates.
6. Place 1 egg in each plate and serve warm.

Nutrition Facts Per Serving:
Calories: 287, Fat: 21.5g, Carbohydrates: 0.9g, Sugar: 0.3g, Protein: 21.4g, Sodium: 1007mg

----

Toad-in-the-Hole Tarts

PREP TIME: 5 MINUTES, COOK TIME: 25 MINUTES, SERVES 4

INGREDIENTS
- 1 sheet frozen puff pastry, thawed and cut into 4 squares
- 30 g cheddar cheese, shredded
- 30 g cooked ham, diced
- 4 eggs
- 2 tbsps. fresh chives, chopped

What you'll need from the store cupboard:
- 15 ml olive oil

DIRECTIONS
1. Preheat the Air fryer to 200 ºC and grease an Air fryer basket.
2. Place 2 pastry squares in the air fryer basket and bake for about 8 minutes.
3. Remove Air fryer basket from the Air fryer and press each square gently with a metal tablespoon to form an indentation.
4. Place 7 g of ham and 7 g of cheddar cheese in each hole and top with 1 egg each.
5. Return Air fryer basket to Air fryer and bake for about 6 more minutes.
6. Remove tarts from the Air fryer basket and allow to cool.
7. Repeat with remaining pastry squares, cheese, ham, and eggs.
8. Dish out and garnish tarts with chives.

Nutrition Facts Per Serving:
Calories: 175, Fat: 13.7g, Carbohydrates: 4.1g, Sugar: 0.5g, Protein: 9.3g, Sodium: 233mg

Breakfast Sausage and Potato Bake

PREP TIME: 10 MINUTES, COOK TIME: 25 MINUTES, SERVES 2

INGREDIENTS
- 3 waxy potatoes
- 3 eggs
- 2 turkey sausage patties
- 30 g cheddar cheese
- 15 ml milk

What you'll need from the store cupboard:
- Olive oil cooking spray

DIRECTIONS
1. Preheat the Air fryer to 200 °C and grease a baking dish with cooking spray.
2. Place the potatoes in the Air fryer basket and air fry for about 10 minutes.
3. Whisk eggs with milk in a bowl.
4. Put the potatoes and sausage in the baking dish and pour egg mixture on top.
5. Sprinkle with cheddar cheese and arrange in the Air fryer.
6. Bake for about 15 minutes at 175 ° C and dish out to serve warm.

Nutrition Facts Per Serving:
Calories: 469, Fat: 16.3g, Carbohydrates: 51.9g, Sugar: 4.1g, Protein: 29.1g, Sodium: 623mg

---

Creamy Chilli Soufflé

PREP TIME: 5 MINUTES, COOK TIME: 10 MINUTES, SERVES 2

INGREDIENTS
- 2 eggs
- 1 tbsp. fresh parsley, chopped
- 1 fresh red chilli pepper, chopped

What you'll need from the store cupboard:
- 30 ml single cream
- Salt, to taste

DIRECTIONS
1. Preheat the Air fryer to 200 ºC and grease 2 soufflé dishes.
2. Mix together all the ingredients in a bowl until well combined.
3. Transfer the mixture into prepared soufflé dishes and place in the Air fryer.
4. Bake for about 10 minutes and dish out to serve warm.

Nutrition Facts Per Serving:
Calories: 108, Fat: 9g, Carbohydrates: 1.1g, Sugar: 0.5g, Protein: 6g, Sodium: 146mg

---

Cheesy Pak Choi and Egg Frittata

PREP TIME: 15 MINUTES, COOK TIME: 8 MINUTES, SERVES 2

INGREDIENTS
- 70 g pak choi, chopped
- 2 eggs
- 30 ml milk
- 7 g cheddar cheese, grated
- 7 g feta cheese, grated

What you'll need from the store cupboard:
- Salt and black pepper, to taste
- 15 ml olive oil
- Cooking spray

DIRECTIONS
1. Preheat the Air fryer to 180 ºC and grease an Air Fryer pan with cooking spray.
2. Whisk together eggs with milk, salt and black pepper in a bowl.
3. Heat olive oil in the Air Fryer pan and add pak choi.
4. Air fry for about 3 minutes and stir in the whisked eggs.
5. Top with cheddar and feta cheese and bake for about 5 minutes.
6. Dish out and serve hot.

Nutrition Facts Per Serving:
Calories: 186, Fat: 11.7g, Carbohydrates: 6.8g, Sugar: 1.7g, Protein: 13.2g, Sodium: 498mg

Eggs, Tomato and Mushrooms Scramble

PREP TIME: 15 MINUTES, COOK TIME: 11 MINUTES, SERVES 4

INGREDIENTS
- 180 ml milk
- 4 eggs
- 8 grape tomatoes, halved
- 35 g mushrooms, sliced
- 1 tbsp. chives, chopped

What you'll need from the store cupboard:
- Salt and black pepper, to taste

DIRECTIONS
1. Preheat the Air fryer to 180 ºC and grease an Air Fryer pan.
2. Whisk eggs with milk, salt, and black pepper in a bowl.
3. Transfer the egg mixture into the Air Fryer pan and cook for about 6 minutes.
4. Add mushrooms, grape tomatoes and chives and air fry for about 5 minutes.
5. Dish out and serve warm.

Nutrition Facts Per Serving:
Calories: 132, Fat: 5.8g, Carbohydrates: 12.5g, Sugar: 9g, Protein: 9.5g, Sodium: 96mg

---

Garlic Tofu and Mushroom Omelette

PREP TIME: 15 MINUTES, COOK TIME: 28 MINUTES, SERVES 2

INGREDIENTS
- ¼ of onion, chopped
- 230 g silken tofu, pressed and sliced
- 100 g fresh mushrooms, sliced
- 3 eggs, beaten
- 30 ml milk

What you'll need from the store cupboard:
- 10 ml rapeseed oil
- 1 garlic clove, minced
- Salt and black pepper, to taste

DIRECTIONS
1. Preheat the Air fryer to 180 ºC and grease an Air Fryer pan.
2. Heat oil in the Air Fryer pan and add garlic and onion.
3. Cook for about 3 minutes and stir in the tofu and mushrooms.
4. Season with salt and black pepper and top with the beaten eggs.
5. Bake for about 25 minutes, poking the eggs twice in between.
6. Dish out and serve warm.

Nutrition Facts Per Serving:
Calories: 224, Fat: 14.5g, Carbohydrates: 6.6g, Sugar: 3.4g, Protein: 17.9g, Sodium: 214mg

---

Sausage Solo

PREP TIME: 5 MINUTES, COOK TIME: 22 MINUTES, SERVES 4

INGREDIENTS
- 6 eggs
- 4 cooked sausages, sliced
- 2 bread slices, cut into sticks
- 58 g mozzarella cheese, grated

What you'll need from the store cupboard:
- 120 ml single cream

DIRECTIONS
1. Preheat the Air fryer to 180 ºC and grease 4 ramekins lightly.
2. Whisk together eggs and cream in a bowl and beat well.
3. Transfer the egg mixture into ramekins and arrange the bread sticks and sausage slices around the edges.
4. Top with mozzarella cheese evenly and place the ramekins in Air fryer basket.
5. Roast for about 22 minutes and dish out to serve warm.

Nutrition Facts Per Serving:
Calories: 180, Fat: 12.7g, Carbohydrates: 3.9g, Sugar: 1.3g, Protein: 12.4g, Sodium: 251mg

Cheddar Breakfast Pockets

PREP TIME: 15 MINUTES, COOK TIME: 30 MINUTES, SERVES 4

INGREDIENTS
- 2 sheets (500 g) puff pastry, cut into 4 equal sized pieces
- 170 g ground breakfast sausage, crumbled
- 2 eggs, lightly beaten
- 115 g cheddar cheese, shredded

What you'll need from the store cupboard:
- 1 tsp. coarse salt
- ½ tsp. ground black pepper
- 30 ml rapeseed oil

DIRECTIONS
1. Preheat the Air fryer to 190 ºC and grease the Air fryer basket.
2. Arrange the sausages in the basket and roast for about 15 minutes.
3. Place the eggs into the basket and air fry for about 5 minutes.
4. Season with salt and black pepper and divide the egg sausages mixture over the 4 puff pastry rectangles.
5. Top with shredded cheddar cheese and drizzle with rapeseed oil.
6. Place 1 egg pocket in the basket and cook for 6 minutes at 200 ºC.
7. Remove from the Air fryer and repeat with the remaining pockets.
8. Serve warm and enjoy.

Nutrition Facts Per Serving:
Calories: 197, Fat: 15.4g, Carbohydrates: 8.5g, Sugar: 1.1g, Protein: 7.9g, Sodium: 203mg

....

Tex-Mex Hash Browns

PREP TIME: 15 MINUTES, COOK TIME: 30 MINUTES, SERVES 4

INGREDIENTS
- 680 g potatoes, peeled, cut into 2.5-cm cubes and soaked
- 1 red bell pepper, seeded and cut into 2.5-cm pieces
- 1 small onion, cut into 2.5-cm pieces
- 1 jalapeno, seeded and cut into 2.5-cm rings

What you'll need from the store cupboard:
- 15 ml olive oil
- ½ tsp. taco seasoning mix
- ½ tsp. ground cumin
- 1 pinch salt and ground black pepper, to taste

DIRECTIONS
1. Preheat the Air fryer to 165 ºC and grease an Air fryer basket.
2. Coat the potatoes with olive oil and transfer into the Air fryer basket.
3. Air fry for about 18 minutes and dish out in a bowl.
4. Mix together bell pepper, onion, and jalapeno in the bowl and season with taco seasoning mix, cumin, salt and black pepper.
5. Toss to coat well and combine with the potatoes.
6. Transfer the seasoned vegetables into the Air fryer basket and air fry for about 12 minutes, stirring in between.
7. Dish out and serve immediately.

Nutrition Facts Per Serving:
Calories: 186, Fat: 4.3g, Carbohydrates: 33.7g, Sugar: 3g, Protein: 4g, Sodium: 79mg

CHAPTER 3
VEGETARIAN AND VEGETABLE RECIPES

Asparagus with Almond / 18

Aromatic Carrots / 18

Broccoli and Cauliflower / 19

Curried Aubergine / 19

Chilli Stuffed Okra / 20

Cumin Butternut Squash / 20

Delightful Mushrooms / 21

Spicy Honey Parsnips / 21

Balsamic Okra with Runner Beans / 22

Hasselback Potatoes / 22

Lemony Runner Beans / 22

Peanut Butter Tofu / 23

Parmesan Stuffed Potatoes / 23

Runner Beans and Button Mushroom Bake / 24

Stuffed Butternut Squash / 24

Tofu with Capers Sauce / 25

Tofu with Orange Sauce / 25

Asparagus with Almond

⏱ *PREP TIME: 15 MINUTES, COOK TIME: 6 MINUTES, SERVES 3*

🍸 INGREDIENTS
- 450 g asparagus
- 25 g almonds, sliced

What you'll need from the store cupboard:
- 60 ml olive oil
- 30 ml balsamic vinegar
- Salt and black pepper, to taste

🍳 DIRECTIONS
1. Preheat the Air fryer to 200 °C and grease an Air fryer basket.
2. Mix asparagus, oil, vinegar, salt, and black pepper in a bowl and toss to coat well.
3. Arrange asparagus into the Air fryer basket and sprinkle with the almond slices.
4. Air fry for about 6 minutes and dish out to serve hot.

Nutrition Facts Per Serving:
Calories: 173, Fat: 14.8g, Carbohydrates: 8.2g, Sugar: 3.3g, Protein: 5.6g, Sodium: 54mg

Aromatic Carrots

⏱ *PREP TIME: 15 MINUTES, COOK TIME: 14 MINUTES, SERVES 8*

🍸 INGREDIENTS
- 6 large carrots, peeled and sliced lengthwise
- 60 ml olive oil
- ½ tbsp. fresh oregano, chopped
- ½ tbsp. fresh parsley, chopped
- Salt and black pepper, to taste

What you'll need from the store cupboard:
- 60 ml olive oil, divided
- 115 ml fat-free Italian dressing
- Salt, to taste

🍳 DIRECTIONS
1. Preheat the Air fryer to 180 °C and grease an Air fryer basket.
2. Mix the carrot slices and olive oil in a bowl and toss to coat well.
3. Arrange the carrot slices in the Air fryer basket and air fry for about 12 minutes.
4. Dish out the carrot slices onto serving plates and sprinkle with herbs, salt and black pepper.
5. Transfer into the Air fryer basket and air fry for 2 more minutes.
6. Dish out and serve hot.

Nutrition Facts Per Serving:
Calories: 93, Fat: 7.2g, Carbohydrates: 7.3g, Sugar: 3.8g, Protein: 0.7g, Sodium: 252mg

Broccoli and Cauliflower

⏱ PREP TIME: 15 MINUTES, COOK TIME: 20 MINUTES, SERVES 4

INGREDIENTS
- 100 g broccoli, cut into 2.5-cm pieces
- 100 g cauliflower, cut into 2.5-cm pieces

What you'll need from the store cupboard:
- 15 ml olive oil
- Salt, as required

DIRECTIONS
1. Preheat the Air fryer to 190 ºC and grease an Air fryer basket.
2. Mix the vegetables, olive oil, and salt in a bowl and toss to coat well.
3. Arrange the veggie mixture in the Air fryer basket and air fry for about 20 minutes, tossing once in between.
4. Dish out in a bowl and serve hot.

Nutrition Facts Per Serving:
Calories: 51, Fat: 3.7g, Carbohydrates: 4.3g, Sugar: 1.5g, Protein: 1.7g, Sodium: 61mg

Curried Aubergine

⏱ PREP TIME: 15 MINUTES, COOK TIME: 10 MINUTES, SERVES 2

INGREDIENTS
- 1 large aubergine, cut into 1-cm thick slices

What you'll need from the store cupboard:
- 1 garlic clove, minced
- ½ fresh red chilli, chopped
- 15 ml rapeseed oil
- ¼ tsp. curry powder
- Salt, to taste

DIRECTIONS
1. Preheat the Air fryer to 150 ºC and grease an Air fryer basket.
2. Mix all the ingredients in a bowl and toss to coat well.
3. Arrange the aubergine slices in the Air fryer basket and air fry for about 10 minutes, tossing once in between.
4. Dish out onto serving plates and serve hot.

Nutrition Facts Per Serving:
Calories: 121, Fat: 7.3g, Carbohydrates: 14.2g, Sugar: 7g, Protein: 2.4g, Sodium: 83mg

Chilli Stuffed Okra

⏱ PREP TIME: 15 MINUTES, COOK TIME: 12 MINUTES, SERVES 2

🍸 **INGREDIENTS**
- 225 g large okra
- 25 g chickpea flour
- ¼ of onion, chopped
- 20 g coconut, grated freshly

What you'll need from the store cupboard:
- 1 tsp. garam masala powder
- ½ tsp. ground turmeric
- ½ tsp. red chilli powder
- ½ tsp. ground cumin
- Salt, to taste

DIRECTIONS
1. Preheat the Air fryer to 200 ºC and grease an Air fryer basket.
2. Mix the flour, onion, grated coconut, and spices in a bowl and toss to coat well.
3. Stuff the flour mixture into okra and arrange into the Air fryer basket.
4. Air fry for about 12 minutes and dish out in a serving plate.

Nutrition Facts Per Serving:
Calories: 166, Fat: 3.7g, Carbohydrates: 26.6g, Sugar: 5.3g, Protein: 7.6g, Sodium: 103mg

Cumin Butternut Squash

⏱ PREP TIME: 15 MINUTES, COOK TIME: 20 MINUTES, SERVES 4

🍸 **INGREDIENTS**
- 1 medium butternut squash, peeled, seeded and cut into chunk
- 2 tsps. cumin seeds
- 15 g pine nuts
- 2 tbsps. fresh coriander, chopped

What you'll need from the store cupboard:
- 1/8 tsp. garlic powder
- 1/8 tsp. chilli flakes, crushed
- Salt and ground black pepper, as required
- 15 ml olive oil

DIRECTIONS
1. Preheat the Air fryer to 190 ºC and grease an Air fryer basket.
2. Mix the squash, spices and olive oil in a bowl.
3. Arrange the butternut squash chunks into the Air fryer basket and air fry for about 20 minutes.
4. Dish out the butternut squash chunks onto serving plates and serve garnished with pine nuts and coriander.

Nutrition Facts Per Serving:
Calories: 165, Fat: 6.9g, Carbohydrates: 27.6g, Sugar: 5.2g, Protein: 3.1g, Sodium: 50mg

Chapter 3: Vegetarian and Vegetable Recipes

Delightful Mushrooms

⏱ *PREP TIME: 20 MINUTES, COOK TIME: 22 MINUTES, SERVES 4*

INGREDIENTS
- 250 g mushrooms, sliced
- 15 g cheddar cheese, shredded
- 1 tbsp. fresh chives, chopped

What you'll need from the store cupboard:
- 60 ml olive oil

DIRECTIONS
1. Preheat the Air fryer to 180 ºC and grease an Air fryer basket.
2. Coat the mushrooms with olive oil and arrange into the Air fryer basket.
3. Air fry for about 20 minutes and dish out in a platter.
4. Top with chives and cheddar cheese and air fry for 2 more minutes.
5. Dish out and serve warm.

Nutrition Facts Per Serving:
Calories: 218, Fat: 7.9g, Carbohydrates: 33.6g, Sugar: 2.5g, Protein: 4.6g, Sodium: 55mg

Spicy Honey Parsnips

⏱ *PREP TIME: 15 MINUTES, COOK TIME: 44 MINUTES, SERVES 6*

INGREDIENTS
- 900 g parsnip, peeled and cut into 2.5-cm chunks
- 15 g butter, melted

What you'll need from the store cupboard:
- 40 g honey
- 1 tbsp. dried parsley flakes, crushed
- ¼ tsp. red pepper flakes, crushed
- Salt and ground black pepper, to taste

DIRECTIONS
1. Preheat the Air fryer to 180 ºC and grease an Air fryer basket.
2. Mix the parsnips and butter in a bowl and toss to coat well.
3. Arrange the parsnip chunks in the Air fryer basket and air fry for about 40 minutes.
4. Mix the remaining ingredients in another large bowl and stir in the parsnip chunks.
5. Transfer the parsnip chunks in the Air fryer basket and air fry for about 4 minutes.
6. Dish out the parsnip chunks onto serving plates and serve hot.

Nutrition Facts Per Serving:
Calories: 155, Fat: 2.4g, Carbohydrates: 33.1g, Sugar: 13g, Protein: 1.9g, Sodium: 57mg

Balsamic Okra with Runner Beans

PREP TIME: 10 MINUTES, COOK TIME: 20 MINUTES, SERVES 2

INGREDIENTS
- 150 g frozen cut okra
- 150 g frozen cut runner beans

What you'll need from the store cupboard:
- 20 g nutritional yeast
- 45 ml balsamic vinegar
- Salt and black pepper, to taste

DIRECTIONS
1. Preheat the Air fryer to 200 ºC and grease an Air fryer basket.
2. Mix the okra, runner beans, nutritional yeast, vinegar, salt, and black pepper in a bowl and toss to coat well.
3. Arrange the okra mixture into the Air fryer basket and air fry for about 20 minutes.
4. Dish out in a serving dish and serve hot.

Nutrition Facts Per Serving:
Calories: 126, Fat: 1.3g, Carbohydrates: 19.7g, Sugar: 2.1g, Protein: 11.9g, Sodium: 100mg

---

Hasselback Potatoes

PREP TIME: 20 MINUTES, COOK TIME: 30 MINUTES, SERVES 4

INGREDIENTS
- 4 potatoes
- 15 g Parmesan cheese, shredded
- 1 tbsp. fresh chives, chopped

What you'll need from the store cupboard:
- 60 ml olive oil

DIRECTIONS
1. Preheat the Air fryer to 180 ºC and grease an Air fryer basket.
2. Cut slits along each potato about ½-cm apart with a sharp knife, making sure slices should stay connected at the bottom.
3. Coat the potatoes with olive oil and arrange into the Air fryer basket.
4. Air fry for about 30 minutes and dish out in a platter.
5. Top with chives and Parmesan cheese to serve.

Nutrition Facts Per Serving:
Calories: 218, Fat: 7.9g, Carbohydrates: 33.6g, Sugar: 2.5g, Protein: 4.6g, Sodium: 55mg

---

Lemony Runner Beans

PREP TIME: 15 MINUTES, COOK TIME: 12 MINUTES, SERVES 3

INGREDIENTS
- 450 g runner beans, trimmed and halved
- 5 g butter, melted

What you'll need from the store cupboard:
- 15 ml fresh lemon juice
- ¼ tsp. garlic powder

DIRECTIONS
1. Preheat the Air fryer to 200 ºC and grease an Air fryer basket.
2. Mix all the ingredients in a bowl and toss to coat well.
3. Arrange the runner beans into the Air fryer basket and air fry for about 12 minutes.
4. Dish out in a serving plate and serve hot.

Nutrition Facts Per Serving:
Calories: 60, Fat: 1.5g, Carbohydrates: 11.1g, Sugar: 2.3g, Protein: 2.8g, Sodium: 70mg

Peanut Butter Tofu

PREP TIME: 20 MINUTES, COOK TIME: 15 MINUTES, SERVES 3

INGREDIENTS

For Tofu:
- 1 (400 g) block tofu, pressed and cut into strips
- 6 bamboo skewers, pre-soaked and halved

What you'll need from the store cupboard:
For Tofu:
- 30 ml fresh lime juice
- 30 ml soy sauce
- 15 ml maple syrup
- 1 tsp. Sriracha sauce
- 2 tsps. fresh ginger, peeled
- 2 garlic cloves, peeled

For Sauce:
- 1 (5-cm) piece fresh ginger, peeled
- 2 garlic cloves, peeled
- 120 g creamy peanut butter
- 15 ml soy sauce
- 15 ml fresh lime juice
- 5-10 ml Sriracha sauce
- 90 ml of water

DIRECTIONS

1. Preheat the Air fryer to 190 ºC and grease an Air fryer basket.
2. Put all the ingredients except tofu in a food processor and pulse until smooth.
3. Transfer the mixture into a bowl and marinate tofu in it.
4. Thread one tofu strip onto each little bamboo stick and arrange them in the Air fryer basket.
5. Air fry for about 15 minutes and dish out onto serving plates.
6. Mix all the ingredients for the sauce in a food processor and pulse until smooth.
7. Drizzle the sauce over tofu and serve warm.

Nutrition Facts Per Serving:
Calories: 385, Fat: 27.3g, Carbohydrates: 9.3g, Sugar: 9.1g, Protein: 23g, Sodium: 1141mg

Parmesan Stuffed Potatoes

PREP TIME: 15 MINUTES, COOK TIME: 31 MINUTES, SERVES 4

INGREDIENTS

- 4 potatoes, peeled
- 15 g butter
- ½ of brown onion, chopped
- 2 tbsps. chives, chopped
- 60 g Parmesan cheese, grated

What you'll need from the store cupboard:
- 45 ml rapeseed oil

DIRECTIONS

1. Preheat the Air fryer to 200 ºC and grease an Air fryer basket.
2. Coat the potatoes with rapeseed oil and arrange into the Air fryer basket.
3. Air fry for about 20 minutes and transfer into a platter.
4. Cut each potato in half and scoop out the flesh from each half.
5. Heat butter in a frying pan over medium heat and add onions.
6. Sauté for about 5 minutes and dish out in a bowl.
7. Mix the onions with the potato flesh, chives, and half of cheese.
8. Stir well and stuff the potato halves evenly with the onion potato mixture.
9. Top with the remaining cheese and arrange the potato halves into the Air fryer basket.
10. Air fry for about 6 minutes and dish out to serve warm.

Nutrition Facts Per Serving:
Calories: 328, Fat: 11.3g, Carbohydrates: 34.8g, Sugar: 3.1g, Protein: 5.8g, Sodium: 77mg

Runner Beans and Button Mushroom Bake

PREP TIME: 15 MINUTES, COOK TIME: 12 MINUTES, SERVES 6

INGREDIENTS
- 680 g fresh runner beans, trimmed
- 250 g fresh button mushrooms, sliced
- 20 g French fried onions

What you'll need from the store cupboard:
- 45 ml olive oil
- 30 ml fresh lemon juice
- 1 tsp. ground sage
- 1 tsp. garlic powder
- 1 tsp. onion powder
- Salt and black pepper, to taste

DIRECTIONS
1. Preheat the Air fryer to 200 °C and grease an Air fryer basket.
2. Mix the runner beans, mushrooms, oil, lemon juice, sage, and spices in a bowl and toss to coat well.
3. Arrange the runner beans mixture into the Air fryer basket and air fry for about 12 minutes.
4. Dish out in a serving dish and top with fried onions to serve.

Nutrition Facts Per Serving:
Calories: 65, Fat: 1.6g, Carbohydrates: 11g, Sugar: 2.4g, Protein: 3g, Sodium: 52mg

Stuffed Butternut Squash

PREP TIME: 20 MINUTES, COOK TIME: 35 MINUTES, SERVES 4

INGREDIENTS
- 2 tomatoes, chopped
- 1 bell pepper, chopped
- 1 beetroot, chopped
- 55 g runner beans, shelled
- ½ of butternut squash, seeded

What you'll need from the store cupboard:
- 2 garlic cloves, minced
- 2 tsps. mixed dried herbs
- Salt and black pepper, to taste

DIRECTIONS
1. Preheat the Air fryer to 180 °C and grease an Air fryer basket.
2. Mix all the ingredients in a bowl except squash and toss to coat well.
3. Stuff the vegetable mixture into the squash and place into the Air fryer basket.
4. Air fry for about 35 minutes and keep aside to slightly cool.
5. Dish out and serve warm.

Nutrition Facts Per Serving:
Calories: 48, Fat: 0.4g, Carbohydrates: 11.1g, Sugar: 5.7g, Protein: 1.8g, Sodium: 25mg

Tofu with Capers Sauce

PREP TIME: 10 MINUTES, COOK TIME: 27 MINUTES, SERVES 4

INGREDIENTS
- 4 tbsps. fresh parsley, divided
- 1 (400 g) block extra-firm tofu, pressed and cut into 8 rectangular cutlets
- 120 g panko breadcrumbs
- 2 tsps. cornflour
- 2 tbsps. capers

What you'll need from the store cupboard:
- 235 ml vegetable broth
- 115 ml lemon juice
- 2 garlic cloves, peeled
- 115 ml mayonnaise
- Salt and black pepper, to taste

DIRECTIONS
1. Preheat the Air fryer to 190 ºC and grease an Air fryer basket.
2. Put half of lemon juice, 2 tbsps. parsley, 2 garlic cloves, salt and black pepper in a food processor and pulse until smooth.
3. Transfer the mixture into a bowl and marinate tofu in it.
4. Place the mayonnaise in a shallow bowl and put the panko breadcrumbs in another bowl.
5. Coat the tofu pieces with mayonnaise and then, roll into the breadcrumbs.
6. Arrange the tofu pieces in the Air fryer pan and air fry for about 20 minutes.
7. Mix broth, remaining lemon juice, remaining garlic, remaining parsley, cornflour, salt and black pepper in a food processor and pulse until smooth.
8. Transfer the sauce into a small pan and stir in the capers.
9. Boil the sauce over medium heat and allow to simmer for about 7 minutes.
10. Dish out the tofu onto serving plates and drizzle with the caper sauce to serve.

Nutrition Facts Per Serving:
Calories: 307, Fat: 15.6g, Carbohydrates: 15.6g, Sugar: 3.4g, Protein: 10.8g, Sodium: 586mg

Tofu with Orange Sauce

PREP TIME: 20 MINUTES, COOK TIME: 20 MINUTES, SERVES 4

INGREDIENTS
- 450 g extra-firm tofu, pressed and cubed
- 115 ml water
- 4 tsps. cornflour, divided
- 2 spring onions (green part), chopped

What you'll need from the store cupboard:
- 115 ml tamari
- 80 ml fresh orange juice
- 20 g honey
- 1 tsp. orange zest, grated
- 1 tsp. garlic, minced
- 1 tsp. fresh ginger, minced
- ¼ tsp. red pepper flakes, crushed

DIRECTIONS
1. Preheat the Air fryer to 200 ºC and grease an Air fryer basket.
2. Mix the tofu, cornflour, and tamari in a bowl and toss to coat well.
3. Arrange half of the tofu pieces in the Air fryer pan and air fry for about 10 minutes.
4. Repeat with the remaining tofu and dish out in a bowl.
5. Put all the ingredients except spring onions in a small pan over medium-high heat and bring to a boil.
6. Pour this sauce over the tofu and garnish with spring onions to serve.

Nutrition Facts Per Serving:
Calories: 148, Fat: 6.7g, Carbohydrates: 13g, Sugar: 6.9g, Protein: 12.1g, Sodium: 263mg

CHAPTER 4
POULTRY RECIPES

BBQ Chicken Wings / 27

Cheesy Spinach Stuffed Chicken Breasts / 27

Chicken and Pepper Kabobs / 28

Curried Chicken and Onion / 28

Easy Turkey Breast / 29

Fried Almond Chicken Thighs / 29

Sweet Chicken Wings / 30

Streaky Rasher Wrapped Chicken Breasts / 30

Beer Coated Duck Breast and Cherry Tomatoes / 31

Chicken with Artichoke Hearts / 31

Delightful Turkey Wings / 32

Crispy Chicken Tenders / 32

Chicken Breasts with Chimichurri / 33

Five-Spice Duck Legs / 33

Jerk Chicken, Pineapple and Veggie Kabobs / 34

Glazed Turkey Breast / 34

Sweet and Sour Chicken Kabobs / 35

Sweet Sriracha Turkey Legs / 35

BBQ Chicken Wings

PREP TIME: 10 MINUTES, COOK TIME: 30 MINUTES, SERVES 4

INGREDIENTS
- 900 g chicken wings, cut into drumettes and flats

What you'll need from the store cupboard:
- 120 ml BBQ sauce

DIRECTIONS
1. Preheat the Air fryer to 195 ºC and grease an Air fryer basket.
2. Arrange the chicken wings into the Air Fryer basket and roast for about 30 minutes.
3. Dish out the chicken wings onto a serving platter and drizzle with the BBQ sauce to serve.

Nutrition Facts Per Serving:
Calories: 478, Fat: 16.9g, Carbohydrates: 11.3g, Sugar: 8.1g, Protein: 65.6g, Sodium: 545mg

---

Cheesy Spinach Stuffed Chicken Breasts

PREP TIME: 15 MINUTES, COOK TIME: 29 MINUTES, SERVES 2

INGREDIENTS
- 50 g fresh spinach
- 65 g ricotta cheese, shredded
- 2 (115 g) skinless, boneless chicken breasts
- 2 tbsps. cheddar cheese, grated

What you'll need from the store cupboard:
- 15 ml olive oil
- Salt and ground black pepper, as required
- ¼ tsp. paprika

DIRECTIONS
1. Preheat the Air fryer to 200 ºC and grease an Air fryer basket.
2. Heat olive oil in a medium frying pan over medium heat and cook spinach for about 4 minutes.
3. Add the ricotta and cook for about 1 minute.
4. Cut the slits in each chicken breast horizontally and stuff with the spinach mixture.
5. Season each chicken breast evenly with salt and black pepper and top with cheddar cheese and paprika.
6. Arrange chicken breasts into the Air fryer basket in a single layer and roast for about 25 minutes.
7. Dish out and serve hot.

Nutrition Facts Per Serving:
Calories: 279, Fat: 16g, Carbohydrates: 2.7g, Sugar: 0.3g, Protein: 31.4g, Sodium: 220mg

Chicken and Pepper Kabobs

⏱ PREP TIME: 20 MINUTES, COOK TIME: 24 MINUTES, SERVES 4

🍲 INGREDIENTS

- 4 (115 g) skinless, boneless chicken thighs, cubed into 2.5-cm size
- 2 bell peppers, cut into 2.5-cm pieces lengthwise
- Wooden skewers, pre-soaked

What you'll need from the store cupboard:
- 60 ml light soy sauce
- 15 ml mirin
- 1 tsp. garlic salt
- 1 tsp. sugar

DIRECTIONS

1. Preheat the Air fryer to 180 ºC and grease an Air fryer pan.
2. Mix the soy sauce, mirin, garlic salt, and sugar in a large baking dish.
3. Thread chicken and bell peppers onto pre-soaked wooden skewers.
4. Coat the skewers generously with marinade and refrigerate for about 3 hours.
5. Transfer the skewers in the Air fryer pan in a single layer and air fry for about 12 minutes.
6. Dish out in a platter and serve warm.

Nutrition Facts Per Serving:
Calories: 161, Fat: 4.1g, Carbohydrates: 6.9g, Sugar: 4g, Protein: 26.2g, Sodium: 781mg

----

Curried Chicken and Onion

⏱ PREP TIME: 15 MINUTES, COOK TIME: 18 MINUTES, SERVES 3

INGREDIENTS

- 450 g boneless chicken, cubed
- ½ tbsp. cornflour
- 1 egg
- 1 medium brown onion, thinly sliced
- 120 ml evaporated milk

What you'll need from the store cupboard:
- 15 ml light soy sauce
- 60 ml olive oil
- 3 tsps. garlic, minced
- 1 tsp. fresh ginger, grated
- 5 curry leaves
- 1 tsp. curry powder
- 1 tbsp. chilli sauce
- 1 tsp. sugar
- Salt and black pepper, as required

DIRECTIONS

1. Preheat the Air fryer to 200 ºC and grease an Air fryer basket.
2. Mix the chicken cubes, soy sauce, cornflour and egg in a bowl and keep aside for about 1 hour.
3. Arrange the chicken cubes into the Air Fryer basket and roast for about 10 minutes.
4. Heat olive oil in a medium frying pan and add onion, garlic, ginger, and curry leaves.
5. Sauté for about 4 minutes and stir in the chicken cubes, curry powder, chilli sauce, sugar, salt, and black pepper.
6. Mix well and add the evaporated milk.
7. Cook for about 4 minutes and dish out the chicken mixture into a serving bowl to serve.

Nutrition Facts Per Serving:
Calories: 363, Fat: 19g, Carbohydrates: 10g, Sugar: 0.8g, Protein: 37.1g, Sodium: 789mg

Easy Turkey Breast

PREP TIME: 20 MINUTES, COOK TIME: 40 MINUTES, SERVES 10

INGREDIENTS
- 1 (3½-kg) bone-in turkey breast

What you'll need from the store cupboard:
- Salt and black pepper, as required
- 60 ml olive oil

DIRECTIONS
1. Preheat the Air fryer to 180 ºC and grease an Air fryer basket.
2. Season the turkey breast with salt and black pepper and drizzle with oil.
3. Arrange the turkey breast into the Air Fryer basket, skin side down and roast for about 20 minutes.
4. Flip the side and roast for another 20 minutes.
5. Dish out in a platter and cut into desired size slices to serve.

Nutrition Facts Per Serving:
Calories: 719, Fat: 35.9g, Carbohydrates: 0g, Sugar: 0g, Protein: 97.2g, Sodium: 386mg

Fried Almond Chicken Thighs

PREP TIME: 10 MINUTES, COOK TIME: 25 MINUTES, SERVES 4

INGREDIENTS
- 50 g almond flour
- 1 egg beaten
- 4 small chicken thighs

What you'll need from the store cupboard:
- 1½ tbsps. Old Bay Cajun Seasoning
- 1 tsp. seasoning salt

DIRECTIONS
1. Preheat the Air fryer to 200 ºC for 3 minutes and grease an Air fryer basket.
2. Whisk the egg in a shallow bowl and place the old bay, flour and salt in another bowl.
3. Dip the chicken in the egg and coat with the flour mixture.
4. Arrange the chicken thighs in the Air fryer basket and air fry for about 25 minutes.
5. Dish out in a platter and serve warm.

Nutrition Facts Per Serving:
Calories: 180, Fat: 20g, Carbohydrates: 3g, Sugar: 1.2g, Protein: 21g, Sodium: 686mg

Chapter 4: Poultry Recipes

Sweet Chicken Wings

⏱ PREP TIME: 20 MINUTES, COOK TIME: 25 MINUTES, SERVES 2

INGREDIENTS
- 2 lemongrass stalk (white portion), minced
- 1 onion, finely chopped
- 450 g chicken wings, rinsed and trimmed
- 60 g cornflour

What you'll need from the store cupboard:
- 15 ml soy sauce
- 30 g honey
- Salt and white pepper, as required

DIRECTIONS
1. Preheat the Air fryer to 180 °C and grease an Air fryer basket.
2. Mix the lemongrass, onion, soy sauce, honey, salt, and white pepper in a bowl.
3. Coat the wings generously with marinade and refrigerate, covered to marinate overnight.
4. Arrange the chicken wings into the Air Fryer basket and roast for about 25 minutes.
5. Dish out the chicken wings onto a serving platter and serve hot.

Nutrition Facts Per Serving:
Calories: 724, Fat: 36.2g, Carbohydrates: 56.9g, Sugar: 15.4g, Protein: 43.5g, Sodium: 702mg

Streaky Rasher Wrapped Chicken Breasts

⏱ PREP TIME: 20 MINUTES, COOK TIME: 23 MINUTES, SERVES 4

INGREDIENTS
- 6-7 Fresh basil leaves
- 30 ml water
- 2 (225 g) chicken breasts, cut each breast in half horizontally
- 12 streaky rashers

What you'll need from the store cupboard:
- 30 ml fish sauce
- 15 g palm sugar
- Salt and ground black pepper, as required
- 1½ tsps. honey

DIRECTIONS
1. Preheat the Air fryer to 185 °C and grease an Air fryer basket.
2. Cook the palm sugar in a small heavy-bottomed pan over medium-low heat for about 3 minutes until caramelized.
3. Stir in the basil, fish sauce and water and dish out in a bowl.
4. Season each chicken breast with salt and black pepper and coat with the palm sugar mixture.
5. Refrigerate to marinate for about 6 hours and wrap each chicken piece with 3 streaky rasher strips.
6. Dip into the honey and arrange into the Air Fryer basket.
7. Roast for about 20 minutes, flipping once in between.
8. Dish out in a serving platter and serve hot.

Nutrition Facts Per Serving:
Calories: 365, Fat: 24.8g, Carbohydrates: 2.7g, Sugar: 2.1g, Protein: 30.2g, Sodium: 1300mg

Beer Coated Duck Breast and Cherry Tomatoes

PREP TIME: 15 MINUTES, COOK TIME: 20 MINUTES, SERVES 2

INGREDIENTS
- 1 tbsp. fresh thyme, chopped
- 235 ml beer
- 1 (300 g) duck breast
- 6 cherry tomatoes

What you'll need from the store cupboard:
- 15 ml olive oil
- 1 tsp. mustard
- Salt and ground black pepper, as required
- 15 ml balsamic vinegar

DIRECTIONS
1. Preheat the Air fryer to 200 ºC and grease an Air fryer basket.
2. Mix the olive oil, mustard, thyme, beer, salt, and black pepper in a bowl.
3. Coat the duck breasts generously with marinade and refrigerate, covered for about 4 hours.
4. Cover the duck breasts and arrange into the Air fryer basket.
5. Roast for about 15 minutes and remove the foil from breast.
6. Set the Air fryer to 180 ºC and place the duck breast and tomatoes into the Air Fryer basket.
7. Roast for about 5 minutes and dish out the duck breasts and cherry tomatoes.
8. Drizzle with vinegar and serve immediately.

Nutrition Facts Per Serving:
Calories: 332, Fat: 13.7g, Carbohydrates: 9.2g, Sugar: 2.5g, Protein: 34.6g, Sodium: 88mg

Chicken with Artichoke Hearts

PREP TIME: 20 MINUTES, COOK TIME: 45 MINUTES, SERVES 2

INGREDIENTS
- 4 small artichoke hearts, quartered
- 4 fresh large button mushrooms, quartered
- ½ small onion, cut in large chunks
- 2 skinless, boneless chicken breasts
- 2 tbsps. fresh parsley, chopped

What you'll need from the store cupboard:
- 2 garlic cloves, minced
- 30 ml chicken broth
- 30 ml red wine vinegar
- 60 ml olive oil
- 1 tbsp. Dijon mustard
- 1/8 tsp. dried thyme
- 1/8 tsp. dried basil
- Salt and black pepper, as required

DIRECTIONS
1. Preheat the Air fryer to 175 ºC and grease a baking dish lightly.
2. Mix the garlic, broth, vinegar, olive oil, mustard, thyme, and basil in a bowl.
3. Place the artichokes, mushrooms, onions, salt, and black pepper in the baking dish.
4. Layer with the chicken breasts and spread half of the mustard mixture evenly on it.
5. Transfer the baking dish into the Air fryer basket and roast for about 23 minutes.
6. Coat the chicken breasts with the remaining mustard mixture and flip the side.
7. Roast for about 22 minutes and serve garnished with parsley.

Nutrition Facts Per Serving:
Calories: 448, Fat: 19.1g, Carbohydrates: 39.1g, Sugar: 5g, Protein: 38.5g, Sodium: 566mg

Delightful Turkey Wings

PREP TIME: 10 MINUTES, COOK TIME: 26 MINUTES, SERVES 4

INGREDIENTS
- 900 g turkey wings

What you'll need from the store cupboard:
- 4 tbsps. chicken rub
- 45 ml olive oil

DIRECTIONS
1. Preheat the Air fryer to 195 °C and grease an Air fryer basket.
2. Mix the turkey wings, chicken rub, and olive oil in a bowl until well combined.
3. Arrange the turkey wings into the Air fryer basket and roast for about 26 minutes, flipping once in between.
4. Dish out the turkey wings in a platter and serve hot.

Nutrition Facts Per Serving:
Calories: 204, Fat: 15.5g, Carbohydrates: 3g, Sugar: 0g, Protein: 12g, Sodium: 465mg

---

Crispy Chicken Tenders

No

PREP TIME: 20 MINUTES, COOK TIME: 30 MINUTES, SERVES 3

INGREDIENTS
- 2 (170 g) boneless, skinless chicken breasts, pounded into 1¼-cm thickness and cut into tenders
- 70 g plain flour
- 180 g panko breadcrumbs
- 60 g Parmesan cheese, finely grated
- 2 large eggs

What you'll need from the store cupboard:
- 1½ tsps. Worcestershire sauce, divided
- 175 ml buttermilk
- ½ tsp. smoked paprika, divided
- Salt and ground black pepper, as required

DIRECTIONS
1. Preheat the Air fryer to 200 °C and grease an Air fryer basket.
2. Mix buttermilk, ¾ tsp. of Worcestershire sauce, ¼ tsp. of paprika, salt, and black pepper in a bowl.
3. Combine the flour, remaining paprika, salt, and black pepper in another bowl.
4. Whisk the egg and remaining Worcestershire sauce in a third bowl.
5. Mix the panko breadcrumbs and Parmesan cheese in a fourth bowl.
6. Put the chicken tenders into the buttermilk mixture and refrigerate overnight.
7. Remove the chicken tenders from the buttermilk mixture and dredge into the flour mixture.
8. Dip into the egg and coat with the breadcrumb mixture.
9. Arrange half of the chicken tenders into the Air Fryer basket and air fry for about 15 minutes, flipping once in between.
10. Repeat with the remaining mixture and dish out to serve hot.

Nutrition Facts Per Serving:
Calories: 537, Fat: 15.5g, Carbohydrates: 50.1g, Sugar: 4.8g, Protein: 48.2g, Sodium: 597mg

Chicken Breasts with Chimichurri

PREP TIME: 15 MINUTES, COOK TIME: 35 MINUTES, SERVES 1

INGREDIENTS
- 1 chicken breast, bone-in, skin-on

Chimichurri:
- ½ bunch fresh coriander
- ¼ bunch fresh parsley
- ½ shallot, peeled, cut in quarters

What you'll need from the store cupboard:
- ½ tbsp. paprika ground
- ½ tbsp. chilli powder
- ½ tbsp. fennel ground
- ½ tsp. black pepper, ground
- ½ tsp. onion powder
- 1 tsp. salt
- ½ tsp. garlic powder
- ½ tsp. cumin ground
- ½ tbsp. rapeseed oil

Chimichurri:
- 60 ml olive oil
- 4 garlic cloves, peeled
- Zest and juice of 1 lemon
- 1 tsp. coarse salt

DIRECTIONS
1. Preheat the Air fryer to 150 ºC and grease an Air fryer basket.
2. Combine all the spices in a suitable bowl and season the chicken with it.
3. Sprinkle with rapeseed oil and arrange the chicken in the Air fryer basket.
4. Air fry for about 35 minutes and dish out in a platter.
5. Put all the ingredients in the blender and blend until smooth.
6. Serve the chicken with chimichurri sauce.

Nutrition Facts Per Serving:
Calories: 140, Fat: 7.9g, Carbohydrates: 1.8g, Sugar: 7.1g, Protein: 7.2g, Sodium: 581mg

---

Five-Spice Duck Legs

PREP TIME: 10 MINUTES, COOK TIME: 30 MINUTES, SERVES 2

INGREDIENTS
- ½ tbsp. fresh thyme, chopped
- ½ tbsp. fresh parsley, chopped
- 2 duck legs

What you'll need from the store cupboard:
- 1 garlic clove, minced
- 1 tsp. five spice powder
- Salt and black pepper, as required

DIRECTIONS
1. Preheat the Air fryer to 170 ºC and grease an Air fryer basket.
2. Mix the garlic, herbs, five spice powder, salt, and black pepper in a bowl.
3. Rub the duck legs with garlic mixture generously and arrange into the Air fryer basket.
4. Air fry for about 25 minutes and set the Air fryer to 200 ºC.
5. Air fry for 5 more minutes and dish out to serve hot.

Nutrition Facts Per Serving:
Calories: 138, Fat: 4.5g, Carbohydrates: 1g, Sugar: 0g, Protein: 25g, Sodium: 82mg

Jerk Chicken, Pineapple and Veggie Kabobs

PREP TIME: 20 MINUTES, COOK TIME: 18 MINUTES, SERVES 8

INGREDIENTS
- 8 (115 g) boneless, skinless chicken thigh fillets, trimmed and cut into cubes
- 2 large courgettes, sliced
- 225 g white mushrooms, stems removed
- 560 g tinned pineapple chunks, drained
- Wooden skewers, pre-soaked

What you'll need from the store cupboard:
- 1 tbsp. jerk seasoning
- Salt and black pepper, to taste
- 15 ml jerk sauce

DIRECTIONS
1. Preheat the Air fryer to 190 ºC and grease an Air fryer pan.
2. Mix the chicken cubes and jerk seasoning in a bowl.
3. Season the courgette slices and mushrooms evenly with salt and black pepper.
4. Thread chicken, courgettes, mushrooms and pineapple chunks onto pre-soaked wooden skewers.
5. Transfer half of the skewers in the Air fryer pan and air fry for about 9 minutes.
6. Repeat with the remaining mixture and dish out to serve hot.

Nutrition Facts Per Serving:
Calories: 274, Fat: 8.7g, Carbohydrates: 14.1g, Sugar: 9.9g, Protein: 35.1g, Sodium: 150mg

---

Glazed Turkey Breast

PREP TIME: 15 MINUTES, COOK TIME: 55 MINUTES, SERVES 8

INGREDIENTS
- 1 (2¼ kg) boneless turkey breast
- 15 g butter, softened

What you'll need from the store cupboard:
- 1 tsp. dried thyme, crushed
- ½ tsp. dried sage, crushed
- ½ tsp. smoked paprika
- Salt and ground black pepper, as required
- 2 tsps. olive oil
- 120 ml maple syrup
- 30 g Dijon mustard

DIRECTIONS
1. Preheat the Air fryer to 175 ºC and grease an Air fryer basket.
2. Mix the herbs, paprika, salt, and black pepper in a bowl.
3. Drizzle the turkey breast with oil and season with the herb mixture.
4. Arrange the turkey breast into the Air Fryer basket and roast for about 50 minutes, flipping twice in between.
5. Meanwhile, mix the maple syrup, mustard, and butter in a bowl.
6. Coat the turkey evenly with maple glaze and roast for about 5 minutes.
7. Dish out the turkey breast onto a cutting board and cut into desired size slices to serve.

Nutrition Facts Per Serving:
Calories: 302, Fat: 3.3g, Carbohydrates: 5.6g, Sugar: 4.7g, Protein: 56.2g, Sodium: 170mg

Sweet and Sour Chicken Kabobs

PREP TIME: 20 MINUTES, COOK TIME: 14 MINUTES, SERVES 3

INGREDIENTS
- 4 spring onions, chopped
- 2 tsps. sesame seeds, toasted
- 450 g chicken tenders
- Wooden skewers, pre-soaked

What you'll need from the store cupboard:
- 1 tbsp. fresh ginger, finely grated
- 4 garlic cloves, minced
- 120 ml pineapple juice
- 120 ml soy sauce
- 60 ml sesame oil
- A pinch of black pepper

DIRECTIONS
1. Preheat the Air fryer to 200 ºC and grease an Air fryer pan.
2. Mix spring onion, ginger, garlic, pineapple juice, soy sauce, oil, sesame seeds, and black pepper in a large baking dish.
3. Thread chicken tenders onto pre-soaked wooden skewers.
4. Coat the skewers generously with marinade and refrigerate for about 2 hours.
5. Transfer half of the skewers in the Air fryer pan and roast for about 7 minutes.
6. Repeat with the remaining mixture and dish out to serve warm.

Nutrition Facts Per Serving:
Calories: 392, Fat: 23g, Carbohydrates: 9.9g, Sugar: 4.1g, Protein: 35.8g, Sodium: 1800mg

Sweet Sriracha Turkey Legs

PREP TIME: 10 MINUTES, COOK TIME: 35 MINUTES, SERVES 2

INGREDIENTS
- 900 g turkey legs
- 15 g butter
- 1 tbsp. fresh coriander
- 1 tbsp. chives
- 1 tbsp. spring onions

What you'll need from the store cupboard:
- 120 ml sriracha sauce
- 20 ml soy sauce
- ½ lime, juiced

DIRECTIONS
1. Preheat the Air fryer on Roasting mode to 180 ºC for 3 minutes and grease an Air fryer basket.
2. Arrange the turkey legs in the Air fryer basket and roast for about 30 minutes, flipping several times in between.
3. Mix butter, spring onions, sriracha sauce, soy sauce and lime juice in the saucepan and air fry for about 3 minutes until the sauce thickens.
4. Drizzle this sauce over the turkey legs and garnish with coriander and chives to serve.

Nutrition Facts Per Serving:
Calories: 361, Fat: 16.3g, Carbohydrates: 9.3g, Sugar: 18.2g, Protein: 33.3g, Sodium: 515mg

CHAPTER 5
FISH AND SEAFOOD RECIPES

Breaded Hake Fillets / 37

Breaded Prawns with Lemon Zest / 37

Buttered Crab Shells / 38

Buttered Sea Scallops / 38

Chilli Panko Prawns / 39

Creamy Tuna Cakes / 39

Garlic Lemon Prawns / 40

Tuna and Celery Cakes / 40

Breaded Flounder with Lemon / 41

Crispy Panko Halibut Strips / 41

Creamy Scallops with Spinach / 41

Lemony Coconut Crusted Salmon / 42

Rice in Crab Shell / 42

Prawn Burgers with Greens / 43

Southern Style Catfish with Mustard / 43

Sesame Seeds Coated Haddock / 44

Wasabi Crab and Celery Cakes / 44

Breaded Hake Fillets

⏱ PREP TIME: 15 MINUTES, COOK TIME: 12 MINUTES, SERVES 2

INGREDIENTS
- 1 egg
- 115 g panko breadcrumbs
- 4 (170 g) hake fillets
- 1 lemon, cut into wedges

What you'll need from the store cupboard:
- 30 ml rapeseed oil

DIRECTIONS
1. Preheat the Air fryer to 175 ºC and grease an Air fryer basket.
2. Whisk the egg in a shallow bowl and mix breadcrumbs and oil in another bowl.
3. Dip hake fillets into the whisked egg and then, dredge in the breadcrumb mixture.
4. Arrange the hake fillets into the Air fryer basket in a single layer and roast for about 12 minutes.
5. Dish out the hake fillets onto serving plates and serve, garnished with lemon wedges.

Nutrition Facts Per Serving:
Calories: 300, Fat: 10.6g, Carbohydrates: 23g, Sugar: 2.2g, Protein: 29.3g, Sodium: 439mg

---

Breaded Prawns with Lemon Zest

⏱ PREP TIME: 15 MINUTES, COOK TIME: 14 MINUTES, SERVES 3

INGREDIENTS
- 70 g plain flour
- 2 egg whites
- 120 g panko breadcrumbs
- 450 g large prawns, peeled and deveined
- Salt and ground black pepper, as required
- ¼ tsp. lemon zest
- ¼ tsp. cayenne pepper
- ¼ tsp. red pepper flakes, crushed

What you'll need from the store cupboard:
- 2 tbsps. rapeseed oil

DIRECTIONS
1. Preheat the Air fryer to 200 ºC and grease an Air fryer basket.
2. Mix flour, salt, and black pepper in a shallow bowl.
3. Whisk the egg whites in a second bowl and mix the breadcrumbs, lime zest and spices in a third bowl.
4. Coat each prawn with the flour, dip into egg whites and finally, dredge in the breadcrumbs.
5. Drizzle the prawns evenly with olive oil and arrange half of the coated prawns into the Air fryer basket.
6. Air fry for about 7 minutes and dish out the coated prawns onto serving plates.
7. Repeat with the remaining mixture and serve hot.

Nutrition Facts Per Serving:
Calories: 432, Fat: 11.3g, Carbohydrates: 44.8g, Sugar: 2.5g, Protein: 37.7g, Sodium: 526mg

Chapter 5: Fish and Seafood Recipes

Buttered Crab Shells

⏱ PREP TIME: 20 MINUTES, COOK TIME: 10 MINUTES, SERVES 4

INGREDIENTS
- 4 soft crab shells, cleaned
- 235 ml buttermilk
- 3 eggs
- 240 g panko breadcrumb
- 30 g butter, melted

What you'll need from the store cupboard:
- 2 tsps. seafood seasoning
- 1½ tsps. lemon zest, grated

DIRECTIONS
1. Preheat the Air fryer to 190 °C and grease an Air fryer basket.
2. Place the buttermilk in a shallow bowl and whisk the eggs in a second bowl.
3. Mix the breadcrumbs, seafood seasoning, and lemon zest in a third bowl.
4. Soak the crab shells into the buttermilk for about 10 minutes, then dip in the eggs.
5. Dredge in the breadcrumb mixture and arrange the crab shells into the Air fryer basket.
6. Air fry for about 10 minutes and dish out in a platter.
7. Drizzle melted butter over the crab shells and immediately serve.

Nutrition Facts Per Serving:
Calories: 521, Fat: 16.8g, Carbohydrates: 11.5g, Sugar: 3.3g, Protein: 47.8g, Sodium: 1100mg

(Note: Seafood Seasoning - Mix the salt, celery seed, dry mustard powder, red pepper, black pepper, bay leaves, paprika, cloves, allspice, ginger, cardamom, and cinnamon together in a bowl until thoroughly combined. Or, you can buy at your local store or on Amazon.)

Buttered Sea Scallops

⏱ PREP TIME: 15 MINUTES, COOK TIME: 4 MINUTES, SERVES 2

INGREDIENTS
- 340 g sea scallops, cleaned and patted very dry
- 15 g butter, melted
- ½ tbsp. fresh thyme, minced

What you'll need from the store cupboard:
- Salt and black pepper, as required

DIRECTIONS
1. Preheat the Air fryer to 200 °C and grease an Air fryer basket.
2. Mix scallops, butter, thyme, salt, and black pepper in a bowl.
3. Arrange scallops in the Air fryer basket and air fry for about 4 minutes.
4. Dish out the scallops in a platter and serve hot.

Nutrition Facts Per Serving:
Calories: 202, Fat: 7.1g, Carbohydrates: 4.4g, Sugar: 0g, Protein: 28.7g, Sodium: 393mg

Chilli Panko Prawns

⏱ PREP TIME: 15 MINUTES, COOK TIME: 20 MINUTES, SERVES 3

INGREDIENTS
- 35 g plain flour
- 120 g panko breadcrumbs
- 450 g prawns, peeled and deveined

What you'll need from the store cupboard:
- 130 g mayonnaise
- 60 g sweet chilli sauce
- 15 g Sriracha sauce

DIRECTIONS
1. Preheat the Air fryer to 200 ºC and grease an Air fryer basket.
2. Place flour in a shallow bowl and mix the mayonnaise, chilli sauce, and Sriracha sauce in another bowl.
3. Place the breadcrumbs in a third bowl.
4. Coat each prawn with the flour, dip into mayonnaise mixture and finally, dredge in the breadcrumbs.
5. Arrange half of the coated prawns into the Air fryer basket and air fry for about 10 minutes.
6. Dish out the coated prawns onto serving plates and repeat with the remaining mixture.

Nutrition Facts Per Serving:
Calories: 540, Fat: 18.2g, Carbohydrates: 33.1g, Sugar: 10.6g, Protein: 36.8g, Sodium: 813mg

---

Creamy Tuna Cakes

⏱ PREP TIME: 15 MINUTES, COOK TIME: 15 MINUTES, SERVES 4

INGREDIENTS
- 2 (170 g) tins tuna, drained
- 22 g almond flour

What you'll need from the store cupboard:
- 20 ml mayonnaise
- 15 ml fresh lemon juice
- 1 tsp. dried dill
- 1 tsp. garlic powder
- ½ tsp. onion powder
- Pinch of salt and ground black pepper

DIRECTIONS
1. Preheat the Air fryer to 200 ºC and grease an Air fryer basket.
2. Mix the tuna, mayonnaise, almond flour, lemon juice, dill, and spices in a large bowl.
3. Make 4 equal-sized patties from the mixture and arrange in the Air fryer basket.
4. Roast for about 10 minutes and flip the sides.
5. Roast for 5 more minutes and dish out the tuna cakes in serving plates to serve warm.

Nutrition Facts Per Serving:
Calories: 200, Fat: 10.1g, Carbohydrates: 2.9g, Sugar: 0.8g, Protein: 23.4g, Sodium: 122mg

Garlic Lemon Prawns

⏱ *PREP TIME: 15 MINUTES, COOK TIME: 8 MINUTES, SERVES 2*

INGREDIENTS
- 340 g medium prawns, peeled and deveined

What you'll need from the store cupboard:
- 20 ml tbsps. fresh lemon juice
- 15 ml olive oil
- 1 tsp. lemon pepper
- ¼ tsp. paprika
- ¼ tsp. garlic powder

DIRECTIONS
1. Preheat the Air fryer to 200 ºC and grease an Air fryer basket.
2. Mix lemon juice, olive oil, lemon pepper, paprika and garlic powder in a large bowl.
3. Stir in the prawns and toss until well combined.
4. Arrange prawns into the Air fryer basket in a single layer and air fry for about 8 minutes.
5. Dish out the prawns in serving plates and serve warm.

Nutrition Facts Per Serving:
Calories: 260, Fat: 12.4g, Carbohydrates: 0.3g, Sugar: 0.1g, Protein: 35.6g, Sodium: 619mg

Tuna and Celery Cakes

⏱ *PREP TIME: 20 MINUTES, COOK TIME: 12 MINUTES, SERVES 4*

INGREDIENTS
- 1 onion, chopped
- 1 green chilli, seeded and finely chopped
- 2 (170 g) tins tuna, drained
- 1 medium rooster potato, boiled and mashed
- 100 g celery
- 120 g panko breadcrumbs
- 2 eggs

What you'll need from the store cupboard:
- ½ tbsp. olive oil
- 1 tbsp. fresh ginger, grated
- Salt, as required

DIRECTIONS
1. Preheat the Air fryer to 200 ºC and grease an Air fryer basket.
2. Heat olive oil in a frying pan and add onions, ginger, and green chilli.
3. Sauté for about 30 seconds and add the tuna.
4. Stir fry for about 3 minutes and dish out the tuna mixture onto a large bowl.
5. Add mashed potato, celery, and salt and mix well.
6. Make 4 equal-sized patties from the mixture.
7. Place the breadcrumbs in a shallow bowl and whisk the egg in another bowl.
8. Dredge each patty with breadcrumbs, then dip into egg and coat again with the breadcrumbs.
9. Arrange tuna cakes into the Air fryer basket and roast for about 3 minutes.
10. Flip the side and roast for about 5 minutes.
11. Dish out the tuna cakes onto serving plates and serve warm.

Nutrition Facts Per Serving:
Calories: 353, Fat: 11.3g, Carbohydrates: 32.6g, Sugar: 3.5g, Protein: 29.1g, Sodium: 302mg

Breaded Flounder with Lemon

PREP TIME: 15 MINUTES, COOK TIME: 12 MINUTES, SERVES 3

INGREDIENTS
- 1 egg
- 120 g dry breadcrumbs
- 3 (170 g) flounder fillets
- 1 lemon, sliced
- What you'll need from the store cupboard:
- 60 ml rapeseed oil

DIRECTIONS
1. Preheat the Air fryer to 180 ºC and grease an Air fryer basket.
2. Whisk the egg in a shallow bowl and mix breadcrumbs and oil in another bowl.
3. Dip flounder fillets into the whisked egg and coat with the breadcrumb mixture.
4. Arrange flounder fillets into the Air fryer basket and air fry for about 12 minutes.
5. Dish out the flounder fillets onto serving plates and garnish with the lemon slices to serve.

Nutrition Facts Per Serving:
Calories: 524, Fat: 24.4g, Carbohydrates: 26.5g, Sugar: 2.5g, Protein: 47.8g, Sodium: 463mg

---

Crispy Panko Halibut Strips

PREP TIME: 20 MINUTES, COOK TIME: 14 MINUTES, SERVES 2

INGREDIENTS
- 2 eggs
- 1 tbsp. water
- 90 g plain panko breadcrumbs
- 350 gras skinless halibut fillets, cut into 2.5-cm strips
- What you'll need from the store cupboard:
- 60 g taco seasoning mix

DIRECTIONS
1. Preheat the Air fryer to 175 ºC and grease an Air fryer basket.
2. Put the taco seasoning mix in a shallow bowl and whisk together eggs and water in a second bowl.
3. Place the breadcrumbs in a third bowl.
4. Dredge the halibut with taco seasoning mix, then dip into the egg mixture and finally, coat evenly with the breadcrumbs.
5. Arrange halibut strips into the Air fryer basket and air fry for about 14 minutes, flipping once in between.
6. Dish out the halibut strips onto serving plates and serve warm.

Nutrition Facts Per Serving:
Calories: 443, Fat: 11.2g, Carbohydrates: 15.5g, Sugar: 0.4g, Protein: 42.4g, Sodium: 961mg

(Note: Taco seasoning mix - Mix chilli powder, garlic powder, onion powder, red pepper flakes, oregano, paprika, cumin, salt and pepper in a small bowl. Store in an airtight container.)

Creamy Scallops with Spinach

PREP TIME: 20 MINUTES, COOK TIME: 10 MINUTES, SERVES 2

INGREDIENTS
- 350 g frozen spinach, thawed and drained
- 8 jumbo sea scallops
- 180 ml double cream
- 1 tbsp. fresh basil, chopped
- What you'll need from the store cupboard:
- Cooking spray
- Salt and ground black pepper, as required
- 1 tbsp. tomato puree
- 1 tsp. garlic, minced

DIRECTIONS
1. Preheat the Air fryer to 175 ºC and grease an Air fryer pan with cooking spray.
2. Season the scallops evenly with salt and black pepper.
3. Mix cream, tomato puree, garlic, basil, salt, and black pepper in a bowl.
4. Place spinach at the bottom of the Air fryer pan, followed by seasoned scallops and top with the cream mixture.
5. Transfer into the Air fryer and air fry for about 10 minutes.
6. Dish out in a platter and serve hot.

Nutrition Facts Per Serving:
Calories: 203, Fat: 18.3g, Carbohydrates: 12.3g, Sugar: 1.7g, Protein: 26.4g, Sodium: 101mg

Lemony Coconut Crusted Salmon

🕐 *PREP TIME: 10 MINUTES, COOK TIME: 6 MINUTES, SERVES 4*

INGREDIENTS
- 450 g salmon
- 70 g plain flour
- 2 egg whites
- 60 g panko breadcrumbs
- 35 g unsweetened coconut, shredded

What you'll need from the store cupboard:
- ¼ tsp. lemon zest
- Salt and freshly ground black pepper, to taste
- ¼ tsp. cayenne pepper
- ¼ tsp. red pepper flakes, crushed
- Rapeseed oil, as required

DIRECTIONS
1. Preheat the Air fryer to 200 ºC and grease an Air fryer basket.
2. Mix the flour, salt and black pepper in a shallow dish.
3. Whisk the egg whites in a second shallow dish.
4. Mix the breadcrumbs, coconut, lime zest, salt and cayenne pepper in a third shallow dish.
5. Coat salmon in the flour, then dip in the egg whites and then into the breadcrumb mixture evenly.
6. Place the salmon in the Air fryer basket and drizzle with rapeseed oil.
7. Roast for about 6 minutes and dish out to serve warm.

Nutrition Facts Per Serving:
Calories: 558, Fat: 22.2g, Carbohydrates: 18.6g, Sugar: 8.7g, Protein: 43g, Sodium: 3456mg

---

Rice in Crab Shell

🕐 *PREP TIME: 20 MINUTES, COOK TIME: 8 MINUTES, SERVES 2*

INGREDIENTS
- 1 bowl cooked rice
- 30 g crab meat
- 30 g butter
- 2 tbsps. Parmesan cheese, shredded
- 2 crab shells

What you'll need from the store cupboard:
- Paprika, to taste

DIRECTIONS
1. Preheat the Air fryer to 200 ºC and grease an Air fryer basket.
2. Mix rice, crab meat, butter and paprika in a bowl.
3. Fill crab shell with rice mixture and top with Parmesan cheese.
4. Arrange the crab shell in the Air fryer basket and air fry for about 8 minutes.
5. Sprinkle with more paprika and serve hot.

Nutrition Facts Per Serving:
Calories: 285, Fat: 33g, Carbohydrates: 0g, Sugar: 0g, Protein: 33g, Sodium: 153mg

Prawn Burgers with Greens

⏱ *PREP TIME: 20 MINUTES, COOK TIME: 6 MINUTES, SERVES 2*

INGREDIENTS
- 160g prawns, peeled, deveined and finely chopped
- 60 g panko breadcrumbs
- 2-3 tbsps. onion, finely chopped
- 180 g fresh baby greens

What you'll need from the store cupboard:
- ½ tsp. ginger, minced
- ½ tsp. garlic, minced
- ½ tsp. spices powder
- ½ tsp. ground cumin
- ¼ tsp. ground turmeric
- Salt and ground black pepper, as required

DIRECTIONS
1. Preheat the Air fryer to 200 ºC and grease an Air fryer basket.
2. Mix the prawns, breadcrumbs, onion, ginger, garlic, and spices in a bowl.
3. Make small-sized patties from the mixture and transfer to the Air fryer basket.
4. Roast for about 6 minutes and dish out in a platter.
5. Serve immediately warm alongside the baby greens.

Nutrition Facts Per Serving:
Calories: 240, Fat: 2.7g, Carbohydrates: 37.4g, Sugar: 4g, Protein: 18g, Sodium: 371mg

---

Southern Style Catfish with Mustard

⏱ *PREP TIME: 15 MINUTES, COOK TIME: 15 MINUTES, SERVES 5*

INGREDIENTS
- 5 (170 g) catfish fillets
- 235 ml milk
- 180 g cornmeal
- 35 g plain flour
- Olive oil cooking spray

What you'll need from the store cupboard:
- 2 tsps. fresh lemon juice
- 125 g mustard
- 2 tbsps. dried parsley flakes
- ¼ tsp. red chilli powder
- ¼ tsp. cayenne pepper
- ¼ tsp. onion powder
- ¼ tsp. garlic powder
- Salt and ground black pepper, as required

DIRECTIONS
1. Preheat the Air fryer to 200 ºC and grease an Air fryer basket.
2. Mix catfish, milk, and lemon juice in a large bowl and refrigerate for about 30 minutes.
3. Put the mustard in a shallow bowl and mix the cornmeal, flour, parsley flakes, and spices in another bowl.
4. Remove the catfish fillets from milk mixture and coat each fish fillet with mustard.
5. Roll evenly into the cornmeal mixture and arrange in the Air fryer basket.
6. Spray with the olive oil cooking spray and air fry for about 10 minutes.
7. Flip the side and air fry for about 5 more minutes.
8. Dish out the catfish fillets onto serving plates and serve hot.

Nutrition Facts Per Serving:
Calories: 340, Fat: 15.5g, Carbohydrates: 18.3g, Sugar: 2.7g, Protein: 30.9g, Sodium: 435mg

Sesame Seeds Coated Haddock

PREP TIME: 15 MINUTES, COOK TIME: 14 MINUTES, SERVES 4

INGREDIENTS
- 35 g plain flour
- 2 eggs
- 70 g sesame seeds, toasted
- 60 g panko breadcrumbs
- 4 (170 g) frozen haddock fillets

What you'll need from the store cupboard:
- 1/8 tsp. dried rosemary, crushed
- Salt and ground black pepper, as required
- 45 ml olive oil

DIRECTIONS
1. Preheat the Air fryer to 200 ºC and grease an Air fryer basket.
2. Place the flour in a shallow bowl and whisk the eggs in a second bowl.
3. Mix sesame seeds, breadcrumbs, rosemary, salt, black pepper and olive oil in a third bowl until a crumbly mixture is formed.
4. Coat each fillet with flour, dip into whisked eggs and finally, dredge into the breadcrumb mixture
5. Arrange haddock fillets into the Air fryer basket in a single layer and roast for about 14 minutes, flipping once in between.
6. Dish out the haddock fillets onto serving plates and serve hot.

Nutrition Facts Per Serving:
Calories: 497, Fat: 24g, Carbohydrates: 20.1g, Sugar: 1.1g, Protein: 49.8g, Sodium: 319mg

Wasabi Crab and Celery Cakes

PREP TIME: 20 MINUTES, COOK TIME: 24 MINUTES, SERVES 6

INGREDIENTS
- 3 spring onions, finely chopped
- 1 celery rib, finely chopped
- 100 g panko breadcrumbs, divided
- 2 large egg whites
- 200 g lump crab meat, drained

What you'll need from the store cupboard:
- 3 tbsps. mayonnaise
- 1 medium red bell pepper, finely chopped
- ¼ tsp. prepared wasabi
- Salt, to taste

DIRECTIONS
1. Preheat the Air fryer to 190 ºC and grease an Air fryer basket.
2. Mix spring onions, red pepper, celery, 40 g of breadcrumbs, egg whites, mayonnaise, wasabi, and salt in a large bowl.
3. Fold in the crab meat gently and mix well.
4. Place the remaining breadcrumbs in another bowl.
5. Make 2-cm thick patties from the mixture and arrange half of the patties into the Air fryer.
6. Roast for about 12 minutes, flipping once halfway through and repeat with the remaining patties.
7. Dish out and serve warm.

Nutrition Facts Per Serving:
Calories: 112, Fat: 4g, Carbohydrates: 15.5g, Sugar: 2.7g, Protein: 4.9g, Sodium: 253mg

CHAPTER 6
BEEF, LAMB AND PORK RECIPES

Cheesy Ham Rolls / 46
Five Spice Pork Belly / 46
Garlic Pork Chops / 47
Italian Sausage Meatballs / 47
Lemony Lamb Loin Chops / 48
Mustard Lamb Loin Chops / 48
Roasted Lamb with Rosemary / 49
Spiced Lamb Sirloin Steaks / 49
Authentic Beef Pot Pie / 50
Beef and Veggie Spring Rolls / 50
Lamb Leg with Brussels Sprouts / 51
Panko Pork Chops / 51
Lamb with Potatoes / 52
Spicy Lamb Kebabs with Pistachios / 52
Mustard Cheesy Beef Meatballs / 52
Simple Lamb Chops / 53
Tomato Stuffed Pork Roll / 53
Veggie Stuffed Beef Rolls with Pesto / 53

Cheesy Ham Rolls

⏱ PREP TIME: 15 MINUTES, COOK TIME: 15 MINUTES, SERVES 4

🏆 INGREDIENTS
- 350 g refrigerated pizza crust, rolled into ½-cm thickness
- 150 g cooked ham, sliced
- 85 g Mozzarella cheese, shredded
- 350 g mild cheddar cheese, shredded
- 85 g roasted red bell peppers

What you'll need from the store cupboard:
- 15 ml olive oil

DIRECTIONS
1. Preheat the Air fryer to 180 °C and grease an Air fryer basket.
2. Arrange the ham, cheeses and roasted peppers over one side of dough and fold to seal.
3. Brush the dough evenly with olive oil and bake for about 15 minutes, flipping twice in between.
4. Dish out in a platter and serve warm.

Nutrition Facts Per Serving:
Calories: 594, Fat: 35.8g, Carbohydrates: 35.4g, Sugar: 2.8g, Protein: 33g, Sodium: 1545mg

- -

Five Spice Pork Belly

⏱ PREP TIME: 15 MINUTES, COOK TIME: 20 MINUTES, SERVES 4

🏆 INGREDIENTS
- 450-g pork belly

What you'll need from the store cupboard:
- 2 tbsps. sugar
- 2 tbsps. dark soy sauce
- 1 tbsp. Shaoxing (cooking wine)
- 2 tsps. garlic, minced
- 2 tsps. ginger, minced
- 1 tbsp. hoisin sauce
- 1 tsp. Chinese Five Spice

DIRECTIONS
1. Preheat the Air fryer to 200 °C and grease an Air fryer basket.
2. Mix all the ingredients in a bowl and place in the zip top bag.
3. Seal the bag, shake it well and refrigerate to marinate for about 1 hour.
4. Remove the pork from the bag and arrange it in the Air fryer basket.
5. Roast for about 15 minutes and dish out in a bowl to serve warm.

Nutrition Facts Per Serving:
Calories: 604, Fat: 30.6g, Carbohydrates: 1.4g, Sugar: 20.3g, Protein: 19.8g, Sodium: 834mg

Chapter 6: Beef, Lamb and Pork Recipes

Garlic Pork Chops

⏱ PREP TIME: 10 MINUTES, COOK TIME: 8 MINUTES, SERVES 4

🏆 INGREDIENTS
- 4 pork chops
- 15 g coconut oil
- 2 tsps. parsley

What you'll need from the store cupboard:
- 1 tbsp. coconut oil
- 2 tsps. garlic, grated
- Salt and black pepper, to taste

🍳 DIRECTIONS
1. Preheat the Air fryer to 175 ºC and grease an Air fryer basket.
2. Mix all the seasonings, coconut oil, garlic, butter, and parsley in a bowl and coat the pork chops with it.
3. Cover the chops with aluminium foil and refrigerate to marinate for about 1 hour.
4. Remove the foil and arrange the chops in the Air fryer basket.
5. Air fry for about 8 minutes and dish out in a bowl to serve warm.

Nutrition Facts Per Serving:
Calories: 311, Fat: 25.5g, Carbohydrates: 1.4g, Sugar: 0.3g, Protein: 18.4g, Sodium: 58mg

• •

Italian Sausage Meatballs

⏱ PREP TIME: 15 MINUTES, COOK TIME: 15 MINUTES, SERVES 4

🏆 INGREDIENTS
- 100 g sausage, casing removed
- ½ medium onion, minced finely
- 1 tsp. fresh sage, chopped finely
- 3 tbsps. panko breadcrumbs

What you'll need from the store cupboard:
- ½ tsp. garlic, minced
- 1 tsp. dry Italian herbs
- Salt and black pepper, to taste

🍳 DIRECTIONS
1. Preheat the Air fryer to 180 ºC and grease an Air fryer basket.
2. Mix all the ingredients in a bowl until well combined.
3. Shape the mixture into equal-sized balls and arrange the balls in the Air fryer basket.
4. Roast for about 15 minutes and dish out to serve warm.

Nutrition Facts Per Serving:
Calories: 111, Fat: 7.3g, Carbohydrates: 5.2g, Sugar: 0.9g, Protein: 5.7g, Sodium: 224mg

Chapter 6: Beef, Lamb and Pork Recipes

Lemony Lamb Loin Chops

⏲ PREP TIME: 10 MINUTES, COOK TIME: 15 MINUTES, SERVES 4

🍷 INGREDIENTS
- 8 (100 g) bone-in lamb loin chops, trimmed
- 15 ml fresh lemon juice
- 5 ml olive oil
- 1 tbsp. Za'atar
- Salt and black pepper, to taste

What you'll need from the store cupboard:
- 3 garlic cloves, crushed

DIRECTIONS
1. Preheat the Air fryer to 200 ºC and grease an Air fryer basket.
2. Mix the garlic, lemon juice, oil, Za'atar, salt, and black pepper in a large bowl.
3. Coat the chops generously with the herb mixture and arrange the chops in the Air fryer basket.
4. Air fry for about 15 minutes, flipping twice in between and dish out the lamb chops to serve hot.

Nutrition Facts Per Serving:
Calories: 433, Fat: 17.6g, Carbohydrates: 0.6g, Sugar: 0.2g, Protein: 64.1g, Sodium: 201mg

(Note: Za'atar - Za'atar is generally made with ground dried thyme, oregano, marjoram, or some combination thereof, mixed with toasted sesame seeds, and salt, though other spices such as sumac might also be added. Some commercial varieties also include roasted flour.)

Mustard Lamb Loin Chops

⏲ PREP TIME: 15 MINUTES, COOK TIME: 30 MINUTES, SERVES 4

🍷 INGREDIENTS
- 8 (115 g) lamb loin chops

What you'll need from the store cupboard:
- 2 tbsps. Dijon mustard
- 15 ml fresh lemon juice
- ½ tsp. olive oil
- 1 tsp. dried tarragon
- Salt and black pepper, to taste

DIRECTIONS
1. Preheat the Air fryer to 200 ºC and grease an Air fryer basket.
2. Mix the mustard, lemon juice, oil, tarragon, salt, and black pepper in a large bowl.
3. Coat the chops generously with the mustard mixture and arrange in the Air fryer basket.
4. Roast for about 15 minutes, flipping once in between and dish out to serve hot.

Nutrition Facts Per Serving:
Calories: 433, Fat: 17.6g, Carbohydrates: 0.6g, Sugar: 0.2g, Protein: 64.1g, Sodium: 201mg

Chapter 6: Beef, Lamb and Pork Recipes

Roasted Lamb with Rosemary

⏲ PREP TIME: 15 MINUTES, COOK TIME: 1 HOUR 30 MINUTES, SERVES 4

INGREDIENTS
- 1¼-kg half lamb leg roast, slits carved
- 2 garlic cloves, sliced into smaller slithers
- 1 tbsp. dried rosemary
- 15 ml olive oil
- Cracked Himalayan rock salt and cracked peppercorns, to taste

What you'll need from the store cupboard:

DIRECTIONS
1. Preheat the Air fryer to 200 °C and grease an Air fryer basket.
2. Insert the garlic slithers in the slits and brush with rosemary, oil, salt, and black pepper.
3. Arrange the lamb in the Air fryer basket and cook for about 15 minutes.
4. Set the Air fryer to 175 °C on the Roast mode and cook for 1 hour and 15 minutes.
5. Dish out the lamb chops and serve hot.

Nutrition Facts Per Serving:
Calories: 246, Fat: 7.4g, Carbohydrates: 9.4g, Sugar: 6.5g, Protein: 37.2g, Sodium: 353mg

Spiced Lamb Sirloin Steaks

⏲ PREP TIME: 15 MINUTES, COOK TIME: 15 MINUTES, SERVES 3

INGREDIENTS
- ½ onion, roughly chopped
- 680 g boneless lamb sirloin steaks

What you'll need from the store cupboard:
- 5 garlic cloves, peeled
- 1 tbsp. fresh ginger, peeled
- 1 tsp. garam masala
- 1 tsp. ground fennel
- ½ tsp. ground cumin
- ½ tsp. ground cinnamon
- ½ tsp. cayenne pepper
- Salt and black pepper, to taste

DIRECTIONS
1. Preheat the Air fryer to 165 °C and grease an Air fryer basket.
2. Put the onion, garlic, ginger, and spices in a blender and pulse until smooth.
3. Coat the lamb steaks with this mixture on both sides and refrigerate to marinate for about 24 hours.
4. Arrange the lamb steaks in the Air fryer basket and roast for about 15 minutes, flipping once in between.
5. Dish out the steaks in a platter and serve warm.

Nutrition Facts Per Serving:
Calories: 252, Fat: 16.7g, Carbohydrates: 4.2g, Sugar: 0.7g, Protein: 21.7g, Sodium: 42mg

Authentic Beef Pot Pie

PREP TIME: 10 MINUTES, COOK TIME: 1 HOUR 27 MINUTES, SERVES 3

INGREDIENTS
- 450 g beef stewing steak, cubed
- 1 can ale mixed into 235 ml water
- 2 beef bouillon cubes
- 1 tbsp. plain flour
- 1 prepared short crust pastry

What you'll need from the store cupboard:
- 15 ml olive oil
- 1 tbsp. tomato puree
- 2 tbsps. onion paste
- Salt and black pepper, to taste

DIRECTIONS
1. Preheat the Air fryer to 200 ºC and grease 2 ramekins lightly.
2. Heat olive oil in a pan and add steak cubes.
3. Cook for about 5 minutes and stir in the onion paste and tomato puree.
4. Cook for about 6 minutes and add the ale mixture, bouillon cubes, salt and black pepper.
5. Bring to a boil and reduce the heat to simmer for about 1 hour.
6. Mix flour and 45 ml of warm water in a bowl and slowly add this mixture into the beef mixture.
7. Roll out the short crust pastry and line 2 ramekins with pastry.
8. Divide the beef mixture evenly in the ramekins and top with extra pastry.
9. Transfer into the Air fryer and cook for about 10 minutes.
10. Set the Air fryer to 170 ºC and roast for about 6 more minutes.
11. Dish out and serve warm.

Nutrition Facts Per Serving:
Calories: 442, Fat: 14.2g, Carbohydrates: 19g, Sugar: 1.2g, Protein: 50.6g, Sodium: 583mg

Beef and Veggie Spring Rolls

PREP TIME: 10 MINUTES, COOK TIME: 35 MINUTES, SERVES 2

INGREDIENTS
- 55 g Asian rice noodles, soaked in warm water, drained and cut into small lengths
- 200 g ground beef
- 1 small onion, chopped
- 70 g fresh mixed vegetables
- 1 packet spring roll skins

What you'll need from the store cupboard:
- 60 ml olive oil
- Salt and black pepper, to taste

DIRECTIONS
1. Preheat the Air fryer to 175 ºC and grease an Air fryer basket.
2. Heat olive oil in a pan and add the onion and garlic.
3. Sauté for about 5 minutes and stir in the beef.
4. Cook for about 5 minutes and add vegetables and soy sauce.
5. Cook for about 7 minutes and stir in the noodles.
6. Place the spring rolls skin onto a smooth surface and put the filling mixture diagonally in it.
7. Fold in both sides to seal properly and brush with oil.
8. Arrange the rolls in batches in the Air fryer basket and air fry for about 13 minutes, tossing in between.
9. Air fry for about 15 minutes, flipping once in between and dish out in a platter.

Nutrition Facts Per Serving:
Calories: 147, Fat: 5.4g, Carbohydrates: 15.9g, Sugar: 0.6g, Protein: 8.7g, Sodium: 302mg

Lamb Leg with Brussels Sprouts

PREP TIME: 20 MINUTES, COOK TIME: 1 HOUR 30 MINUTES, SERVES 6

INGREDIENTS
- 1 kg leg of lamb
- 1 tbsp. fresh rosemary, minced
- 1 tbsp. fresh lemon thyme
- 680 g Brussels sprouts, trimmed

What you'll need from the store cupboard:

- 45 ml olive oil, divided
- 1 garlic clove, minced
- Salt and ground black pepper, as required
- 40 g honey

DIRECTIONS
1. Preheat the Air fryer to 150 ºC and grease an Air fryer basket.
2. Make slits in the leg of lamb with a sharp knife.
3. Mix 30 ml of oil, herbs, garlic, salt, and black pepper in a bowl.
4. Coat the leg of lamb with oil mixture generously and arrange in the Air fryer basket.
5. Roast for about 75 minutes and set the Air fryer to 200 ºC.
6. Coat the Brussels sprouts evenly with the remaining oil and honey and arrange them in the Air fryer basket with leg of lamb.
7. Air fry for about 15 minutes and dish out to serve warm.

Nutrition Facts Per Serving:
Calories: 449, Fat: 19.9g, Carbohydrates: 16.6g, Sugar: 8.2g, Protein: 51.7g, Sodium: 185mg

Panko Pork Chops

PREP TIME: 15 MINUTES, COOK TIME: 15 MINUTES, SERVES 2

INGREDIENTS
- 2 (170 g) pork chops
- 35 g plain flour
- 1 egg
- 115 g Panko breadcrumbs

What you'll need from the store cupboard:
- Salt and black pepper, to taste
- 15 ml rapeseed oil

DIRECTIONS
1. Preheat the Air fryer to 200 ºC and grease an Air fryer basket.
2. Season the chops with salt and black pepper.
3. Place the flour in a shallow bowl and whisk an egg in a second bowl.
4. Mix the breadcrumbs and rapeseed oil in a third bowl.
5. Coat the pork chops with flour, dip into egg and dredge into the breadcrumb mixture.
6. Arrange the chops in the Air fryer basket and roast for about 15 minutes, flipping once in between.
7. Dish out and serve hot.

Nutrition Facts Per Serving:
Calories: 621, Fat: 26.1g, Carbohydrates: 53.3g, Sugar: 3.7g, Protein: 43.9g, Sodium: 963mg

Lamb with Potatoes

PREP TIME: 20 MINUTES, COOK TIME: 35 MINUTES, SERVES 2

INGREDIENTS
- 230 g lamb meat
- 2 small potatoes, peeled and halved
- ½ small onion, peeled and halved
- 15 g frozen sweet potato chips

What you'll need from the store cupboard:
- 1 garlic clove, crushed
- ½ tbsp. dried rosemary, crushed
- 5 ml olive oil

DIRECTIONS
1. Preheat the Air fryer to 180 ºC and arrange a divider in the Air fryer.
2. Rub the lamb evenly with garlic and rosemary and place on one side of Air fryer divider.
3. Roast for about 20 minutes and meanwhile, microwave the potatoes for about 4 minutes.
4. Dish out the potatoes in a large bowl and stir in the olive oil and onions.
5. Transfer into the Air fryer divider and change the side of lamb ramp.
6. Air fry for about 15 minutes, flipping once in between and dish out in a bowl.

Nutrition Facts Per Serving:
Calories: 399, Fat: 18.5g, Carbohydrates: 32.3g, Sugar: 3.8g, Protein: 24.5g, Sodium: 104mg

---

Spicy Lamb Kebabs with Pistachios

PREP TIME: 20 MINUTES, COOK TIME: 8 MINUTES, SERVES 6

INGREDIENTS
- 4 eggs, beaten
- 150 g pistachios, chopped
- 450 g ground lamb
- 35 g plain flour
- 4 tbsps. flat-leaf parsley, chopped

What you'll need from the store cupboard:
- 2 tsps. chilli flakes
- 4 garlic cloves, minced
- 30 ml fresh lemon juice
- 2 tsps. cumin seeds
- 1 tsp. fennel seeds
- 2 tsps. dried mint
- 2 tsps. salt
- Olive oil
- 1 tsp. coriander seeds
- 1 tsp. freshly ground black pepper

DIRECTIONS
1. Preheat the Air fryer to 180 ºC and grease an Air fryer basket.
2. Mix lamb, pistachios, eggs, lemon juice, chilli flakes, flour, cumin seeds, fennel seeds, coriander seeds, mint, parsley, salt and black pepper in a large bowl.
3. Thread the lamb mixture onto metal skewers to form sausages and coat with olive oil.
4. Place the skewers in the Air fryer basket and roast for about 8 minutes.
5. Dish out in a platter and serve hot.

Nutrition Facts Per Serving:
Calories: 284, Fat: 15.8g, Carbohydrates: 8.4g, Sugar: 1.1g, Protein: 27.9g, Sodium: 932mg

---

Mustard Cheesy Beef Meatballs

PREP TIME: 15 MINUTES, COOK TIME: 15 MINUTES, SERVES 6

INGREDIENTS
- 2 onions, chopped
- 450 g ground beef
- 4 tbsps. fresh basil, chopped
- 15 g cheddar cheese, grated

What you'll need from the store cupboard:
- 2 tsps. garlic paste
- 15 g honey
- Salt and black pepper, to taste
- 2 tsps. mustard

DIRECTIONS
1. Preheat the Air fryer to 385 ºC and grease an Air fryer basket.
2. Mix all the ingredients in a bowl until well combined.
3. Shape the mixture into equal-sized balls gently and arrange the meatballs in the Air fryer basket.
4. Air fry for about 15 minutes and dish out to serve warm.

Nutrition Facts Per Serving:
Calories: 134, Fat: 4.4g, Carbohydrates: 4.6g, Sugar: 2.7g, Protein: 18.2g, Sodium: 50mg

Simple Lamb Chops

🕐 *PREP TIME: 10 MINUTES, COOK TIME: 15 MINUTES, SERVES 2*

🏆 INGREDIENTS
- 4 (115 g) lamb chops
  What you'll need from the store cupboard:
- Salt and black pepper, to taste
- 15 ml olive oil

🍳 DIRECTIONS
1. Preheat the Air fryer to 200 ºC and grease an Air fryer basket.
2. Mix the olive oil, salt, and black pepper in a large bowl and add chops.
3. Arrange the chops in the Air fryer basket and roast for about 15 minutes.
4. Dish out the lamb chops and serve hot.

Nutrition Facts Per Serving:
Calories: 486, Fat: 31.7g, Carbohydrates: 0.8g, Sugar: 0g, Protein: 63.8g, Sodium: 250mg

....

Tomato Stuffed Pork Roll

🕐 *PREP TIME: 20 MINUTES, COOK TIME: 15 MINUTES, SERVES 4*

🏆 INGREDIENTS
- 1 spring onion, chopped
- 15 g sun-dried tomatoes, chopped finely
- 2 tbsps. fresh parsley, chopped
- 4 (170 g) pork cutlets, pounded slightly

What you'll need from the store cupboard:
- Salt and freshly ground black pepper, to taste
- 2 tsps. paprika
- 7 ml olive oil

🍳 DIRECTIONS
1. Preheat the Air fryer to 200 ºC and grease an Air fryer basket.
2. Mix spring onion, tomatoes, parsley, salt and black pepper in a bowl.
3. Coat each cutlet with tomato mixture and roll up the cutlet, securing with cocktail sticks.
4. Coat the rolls with oil and rub with paprika, salt and black pepper.
5. Arrange the rolls in the Air fryer basket and air fry for about 15 minutes, flipping once in between.
6. Dish out in a platter and serve warm.

Nutrition Facts Per Serving:
Calories: 244, Fat: 14.5g, Carbohydrates: 20.1g, Sugar: 1.7g, Protein: 8.2g, Sodium: 670mg

....

Veggie Stuffed Beef Rolls with Pesto

🕐 *PREP TIME: 20 MINUTES, COOK TIME: 14 MINUTES, SERVES 6*

🏆 INGREDIENTS
- 900 g beef flank steak, pounded to ¼-cm thickness
- 6 Provolone cheese slices
- 85 g roasted red bell peppers
- 25 g fresh baby spinach

What you'll need from the store cupboard:
- 45 g prepared pesto
- Salt and black pepper, to taste

🍳 DIRECTIONS
1. Preheat the Air fryer to 200 ºC and grease an Air fryer basket.
2. Place the steak onto a smooth surface and spread evenly with pesto.
3. Top with the cheese slices, red peppers and spinach.
4. Roll up the steak tightly around the filling and secure with the toothpicks.
5. Arrange the roll in the Air fryer basket and air fry for about 14 minutes, flipping once in between.
6. Dish out in a platter and serve warm.

Nutrition Facts Per Serving:
Calories: 447, Fat: 23.4g, Carbohydrates: 1.8g, Sugar: 0.6g, Protein: 53.2g, Sodium: 472mg

CHAPTER 7
SNACKS RECIPES

Buttered Bread Rolls / 55

Cheese Stuffed Mushrooms / 55

Crispy Avocado Chips / 56

Croissant Rolls / 56

Crispy Prawns / 57

Hot Cauliflower Poppers / 57

Mozzarella Sticks / 58

Spicy Chilli Broccoli Poppers / 58

Cheese Broccoli Stuffed Tomatoes / 59

Fluffy Sunflower Seeds Bread / 59

Healthy Pumpkin and Tomato Lasagne / 59

Heirloom Tomato Sandwiches with Pesto / 60

Radish Sticks / 60

Rice Flour Crusted Tofu / 60

Stuffed Mushrooms with Carrot / 61

Spiced Soya Curls / 61

Streaky Rasher Filled Poppers / 61

Buttered Bread Rolls

PREP TIME: 15 MINUTES, COOK TIME: 30 MINUTES, SERVES 12

INGREDIENTS
- 235 ml milk
- 405 g plain flour
- 115 g unsalted butter

What you'll need from the store cupboard:
- 15 g coconut oil
- 15 ml olive oil
- 1 tsp. yeast
- Salt and black pepper, to taste

DIRECTIONS
1. Preheat the Air fryer to 180 ºC and grease an Air fryer basket.
2. Put olive oil, milk and coconut oil in a pan and cook for about 3 minutes.
3. Remove from the heat and mix well.
4. Mix together plain flour, yeast, butter, salt and black pepper in a large bowl.
5. Knead well for about 5 minutes until a dough is formed.
6. Cover the dough with a damp cloth and keep aside for about 5 minutes in a warm place.
7. Knead the dough for about 5 minutes again with your hands.
8. Cover the dough with a damp cloth and keep aside for about 30 minutes in a warm place.
9. Divide the dough into 12 equal pieces and roll each into a ball.
10. Arrange 6 balls into the Air fryer basket in a single layer and bake for about 15 minutes.
11. Repeat with the remaining balls and serve warm.

Nutrition Facts Per Serving:
Calories: 208, Fat: 10.3g, Carbohydrates: 25g, Sugar: 1g, Protein: 4.1g, Sodium: 73mg

Cheese Stuffed Mushrooms

PREP TIME: 15 MINUTES, COOK TIME: 8 MINUTES, SERVES 4

INGREDIENTS
- 4 fresh large mushrooms, stemmed and gills removed
- 30 g Parmesan cheese, shredded
- 15 g white cheddar cheese, shredded
- 15 g sharp cheddar cheese, shredded

What you'll need from the store cupboard:
- Salt and black pepper, to taste
- 80 ml rapeseed oil
- 115 g cream cheese, softened
- 5 ml Worcestershire sauce
- 2 garlic cloves, chopped
- Salt and ground black pepper, as required

DIRECTIONS
1. Preheat the Air fryer to 190 ºC and grease an Air fryer basket.
2. Mix together Parmesan cheese, cheddar cheese, Worcestershire sauce, cream cheese, garlic, salt and black pepper in a bowl,
3. Stuff the cheese mixture in each mushroom and arrange in the Air fryer basket.
4. Air fry for about 8 minutes and dish out in a serving platter.

Nutrition Facts Per Serving:
Calories: 156, Fat: 13.6g, Carbohydrates: 2.6g, Sugar: 0.7g, Protein: 6.5g, Sodium: 267mg

Chapter 7: Snacks Recipes

Crispy Avocado Chips

⏱ PREP TIME: 20 MINUTES, COOK TIME: 7 MINUTES, SERVES 2

🏆 INGREDIENTS
- 35 g plain flour
- 1 egg
- 5 ml water
- 60 g panko breadcrumbs
- 1 avocado, peeled, pitted and sliced into 8 pieces

What you'll need from the store cupboard:
- Salt and black pepper, to taste

DIRECTIONS
1. Preheat the Air fryer to 200 ºC and grease an Air fryer basket.
2. Place flour, salt and black pepper in a shallow dish and whisk the egg with water in a second dish.
3. Place the breadcrumbs in a third shallow dish.
4. Coat the avocado slices evenly in flour and dip in the egg mixture.
5. Roll into the breadcrumbs evenly and arrange the avocado slices in an Air fryer basket.
6. Air fry for about 7 minutes, flipping once in between and dish out to serve warm.

Nutrition Facts Per Serving:
Calories: 363, Fat: 22.4g, Carbohydrates: 35.7g, Sugar: 1.2g, Protein: 8.3g, Sodium: 225mg

---

Croissant Rolls

⏱ PREP TIME: 10 MINUTES, COOK TIME: 6 MINUTES, SERVES 8

🏆 INGREDIENTS
- 1 (225 g) can croissant rolls
- 60 g butter, melted

What you'll need from the store cupboard:
- 15 ml olive oil

DIRECTIONS
1. Preheat the Air fryer to 160 ºC and grease an Air fryer basket with olive oil.
2. Coat the croissant rolls with butter and arrange into the Air fryer basket.
3. Bake for about 6 minutes, flipping once in between.
4. Dish out in a platter and serve hot.

Nutrition Facts Per Serving:
Calories: 167, Fat: 12.6g, Carbohydrates: 11.1g, Sugar: 3g, Protein: 2.1g, Sodium: 223mg

Chapter 7: Snacks Recipes

Crispy Prawns

⏲ PREP TIME: 15 MINUTES, COOK TIME: 8 MINUTES, SERVES 2

INGREDIENTS
- 1 egg
- 115 g nacho crisps, crushed
- 10 prawns, peeled and deveined

What you'll need from the store cupboard:
- 15 ml olive oil
- Salt and black pepper, to taste

DIRECTIONS
1. Preheat the Air fryer to 185 ºC and grease an Air fryer basket.
2. Crack egg in a shallow dish and beat well.
3. Place the nacho crisps in another shallow dish.
4. Season the prawns with salt and black pepper, coat into egg and then roll into nacho crisps.
5. Place the coated prawns into the Air fryer basket and air fry for about 8 minutes.
6. Dish out and serve warm.

Nutrition Facts Per Serving:
Calories: 514, Fat: 25.8g, Carbohydrates: 36.9g, Sugar: 2.3g, Protein: 32.5g, Sodium: 648mg

---

Hot Cauliflower Poppers

⏲ PREP TIME: 10 MINUTES, COOK TIME: 20 MINUTES, SERVES 4

INGREDIENTS
- 1 large egg white
- 90 g panko breadcrumbs
- 280 g cauliflower florets

What you'll need from the store cupboard:
- 45 ml ketchup
- 30 ml hot sauce

DIRECTIONS
1. Preheat the Air fryer to 160 ºC and grease an Air fryer basket.
2. Mix together the egg white, ketchup, and hot sauce in a bowl until well combined.
3. Stir in the cauliflower florets and generously coat with marinade.
4. Place breadcrumbs in a shallow dish and dredge the cauliflower florets in it.
5. Arrange the cauliflower florets in the Air fryer basket and air fry for about 20 minutes, flipping once in between.
6. Dish out and serve warm.

Nutrition Facts Per Serving:
Calories: 94, Fat: 0.5g, Carbohydrates: 19.6g, Sugar: 5.5g, Protein: 4.6g, Sodium: 457mg

Mozzarella Sticks

⏱ PREP TIME: 4 HOURS, COOK TIME: 12 MINUTES, SERVES 4

INGREDIENTS
- 35 g plain flour
- 2 eggs
- 45 ml non-fat milk
- 120 g panko breadcrumbs
- 450 g Mozzarella cheese block, cut into 7½x1-cm sticks

What you'll need from the store cupboard:
- Salt and black pepper, to taste

DIRECTIONS
1. Preheat the Air fryer to 225 °C and grease an Air fryer basket.
2. Place flour in a shallow dish and whisk the eggs with milk, salt and black pepper in a second dish.
3. Place breadcrumbs in a third shallow dish.
4. Coat the Mozzarella sticks with flour, then dip into egg mixture and finally, dredge in the breadcrumbs.
5. Arrange the Mozzarella sticks on a baking sheet and freeze for about 4 hours.
6. Transfer into the Air fryer and air fry for about 12 minutes.
7. Dish out in a platter and serve warm.

Nutrition Facts Per Serving:
Calories: 191, Fat: 5g, Carbohydrates: 26.4g, Sugar: 2.4g, Protein: 9.6g, Sodium: 177mg

---

Spicy Chilli Broccoli Poppers

⏱ PREP TIME: 35 MINUTES, COOK TIME: 10 MINUTES, SERVES 4

INGREDIENTS
- 30 g plain yoghurt
- 450 g broccoli, cut into small florets
- 18 g chickpea flour
- ½ tsp. red chilli powder
- ¼ tsp. ground cumin
- ¼ tsp. ground turmeric
- Salt, to taste

What you'll need from the store cupboard:

DIRECTIONS
1. Preheat the Air fryer to 200 °C and grease an Air fryer basket.
2. Mix together the yoghurt, red chilli powder, cumin, turmeric and salt in a bowl until well combined.
3. Stir in the broccoli and generously coat with marinade.
4. Refrigerate for about 30 minutes and sprinkle the broccoli florets with chickpea flour.
5. Arrange the broccoli florets in the Air fryer basket and air fry for about 10 minutes, flipping once in between.
6. Dish out and serve warm.

Nutrition Facts Per Serving:
Calories: 69, Fat: 0.9g, Carbohydrates: 12.2g, Sugar: 3.2g, Protein: 4.9g, Sodium: 87mg

Chapter 7: Snacks Recipes

Cheese Broccoli Stuffed Tomatoes

PREP TIME: 15 MINUTES, COOK TIME: 15 MINUTES, SERVES 2

INGREDIENTS
- 2 large tomatoes, sliced in half and pulp scooped out
- 35 g broccoli, finely chopped
- 60 g cheddar cheese, shredded
- 15 g unsalted butter, melted

What you'll need from the store cupboard:
- ½ tsp. dried thyme, crushed

DIRECTIONS
1. Preheat the Air fryer to 180 ºC and grease an Air fryer basket.
2. Mix together broccoli and cheese in a bowl.
3. Stuff the broccoli mixture in each tomato.
4. Arrange the stuffed tomatoes into the Air fryer basket and drizzle evenly with butter.
5. Air fry for about 15 minutes and dish out in a serving platter.
6. Garnish with thyme and serve warm.

Nutrition Facts Per Serving:
Calories: 206, Fat: 15.6g, Carbohydrates: 9.1g, Sugar: 5.3g, Protein: 9.4g, Sodium: 233mg

---

Fluffy Sunflower Seeds Bread

PREP TIME: 15 MINUTES, COOK TIME: 18 MINUTES, SERVES 4

INGREDIENTS
- 90 g fine wholemeal flour
- 90 g plain flour
- 45 g sunflower seeds
- 235 ml lukewarm water

What you'll need from the store cupboard:
- ½ sachet instant yeast
- 1 tsp. salt

DIRECTIONS
1. Preheat the Air fryer to 200 ºC and grease a cake pan.
2. Mix together flours, sunflower seeds, yeast and salt in a bowl.
3. Add water slowly and knead for about 5 minutes until a dough is formed.
4. Cover the dough with a clingfilm and keep in warm place for about half an hour.
5. Arrange the dough into a cake pan and transfer into an Air fryer basket.
6. Bake for about 18 minutes and dish out to serve warm.

Nutrition Facts Per Serving:
Calories: 156, Fat: 2.4g, Carbohydrates: 28.5g, Sugar: 0.5g, Protein: 4.6g, Sodium: 582mg

---

Healthy Pumpkin and Tomato Lasagne

PREP TIME: 15 MINUTES, COOK TIME: 1 HOUR, SERVES 4

INGREDIENTS
- 680 g pumpkin, peeled and chopped finely
- 340 g tomatoes, cubed
- 450 g cooked beetroots, sliced thinly
- 230 g fresh lasagne sheets
- 30 g Parmesan cheese, grated

What you'll need from the store cupboard:
- 30 ml sunflower oil

DIRECTIONS
1. Preheat the Air fryer to 150 ºC and lightly grease a baking dish.
2. Put pumpkin and 15 ml sunflower oil in a frying pan and cook for about 10 minutes.
3. Put the pumpkin mixture and tomatoes in a blender and pulse until smooth.
4. Return to the frying pan and cook on low heat for about 5 minutes.
5. Transfer the pumpkin puree into the baking dish and layer with lasagne sheets.
6. Top with the beetroot slices and cheese and place in the Air fryer.
7. Air fry for about 45 minutes and dish out to serve warm.

Nutrition Facts Per Serving:
Calories: 368, Fat: 10.3g, Carbohydrates: 59.8g, Sugar: 16.9g, Protein: 13.4g, Sodium: 165mg

Heirloom Tomato Sandwiches with Pesto

PREP TIME: 20 MINUTES, COOK TIME: 16 MINUTES, SERVES 4

INGREDIENTS
- 25 g pine nuts
- 30 g fresh basil, chopped
- 30 g fresh parsley, chopped
- 2 heirloom tomatoes, cut into 1-cm thick slices
- 115 g feta cheese, cut into 1-cm thick slices

What you'll need from the store cupboard:
- 180 ml olive oil, divided
- Salt, to taste
- 1 garlic clove, chopped

DIRECTIONS
1. Preheat the Air fryer to 200 ºC and grease an Air fryer basket.
2. Mix together 15 ml of olive oil, pine nuts and pinch of salt in a bowl.
3. Place pine nuts in the Air fryer and cook for about 2 minutes.
4. Put the pine nuts, remaining oil, fresh basil, fresh parsley, garlic and salt and pulse until combined.
5. Dish out the pesto in a bowl, cover and refrigerate.
6. Spread 15 ml of pesto on each tomato slice and top with a feta slice and onion.
7. Drizzle with olive oil and arrange the prepared tomato slices in the Air fryer basket.
8. Bake for about 14 minutes and serve with remaining pesto.

Nutrition Facts Per Serving:
Calories: 559, Fat: 55.7g, Carbohydrates: 8g, Sugar: 2.6g, Protein: 11.8g, Sodium: 787mg

---

Radish Sticks

PREP TIME: 10 MINUTES, COOK TIME: 12 MINUTES, SERVES 2

INGREDIENTS
- 1 large radish, peeled and cut into sticks
- 1 tbsp. fresh rosemary, finely chopped

What you'll need from the store cupboard:
- 15 ml olive oil
- 2 tsps. sugar
- ¼ tsp. cayenne pepper
- Salt and black pepper, as needed

DIRECTIONS
1. Preheat the Air fryer to 200 ºC and grease an Air fryer basket.
2. Mix radish with all other ingredients in a bowl until well combined.
3. Arrange the radish sticks in the Air fryer basket and air fry for about 12 minutes.
4. Dish out and serve warm.

Nutrition Facts Per Serving:
Calories: 96, Fat: 7.3g, Carbohydrates: 8.7g, Sugar: 5.8g, Protein: 0.4g, Sodium: 26mg

---

Rice Flour Crusted Tofu

PREP TIME: 15 MINUTES, COOK TIME: 28 MINUTES, SERVES 3

INGREDIENTS
- 1 (400-g) block firm tofu, pressed and cubed into 1-cm size
- 15 g cornflour
- 40 g rice flour

What you'll need from the store cupboard:
- Salt and ground black pepper, as required
- 60 ml olive oil

DIRECTIONS
1. Preheat the Air fryer to 180 ºC and grease an Air fryer basket.
2. Mix together cornflour, rice flour, salt, and black pepper in a bowl.
3. Coat the tofu with flour mixture evenly and drizzle with olive oil.
4. Arrange the tofu cubes into the Air fryer basket and air fry for about 28 minutes.
5. Dish out the tofu in a serving platter and serve warm.

Nutrition Facts Per Serving:
Calories: 241, Fat: 15g, Carbohydrates: 17.7g, Sugar: 0.8g, Protein: 11.6g, Sodium: 67mg

Stuffed Mushrooms with Carrot

⏱ *PREP TIME: 15 MINUTES, COOK TIME: 13 MINUTES, SERVES 12*

INGREDIENTS
- ¼ orange bell pepper, diced
- 85 g Cheddar cheese, shredded
- 12 mushroom caps, stems diced
- ½ onion, diced
- ½ small carrot, diced

What you'll need from the store cupboard:
- 60 ml sour cream

DIRECTIONS
1. Preheat the Air fryer to 175 ºC and grease a baking tray.
2. Place mushroom stems, onion, orange bell pepper and carrot over medium heat in a frying pan.
3. Cook for about 5 minutes until softened and stir in 60 g of Cheddar cheese and sour cream.
4. Stuff this mixture in the mushroom caps and arrange them on the baking tray.
5. Top with rest of the cheese and place the baking tray in the Air fryer basket.
6. Air fry for about 8 minutes until cheese is melted and serve warm.

Nutrition Facts Per Serving:
Calories: 43, Fat: 3.1g, Carbohydrates: 1.7g, Sugar: 1g, Protein: 2.4g, Sodium: 55mg

---

Spiced Soya Curls

⏱ *PREP TIME: 15 MINUTES, COOK TIME: 10 MINUTES, SERVES 2*

INGREDIENTS
- 115 g soya curls, soaked in boiling water for about 10 minutes and drained
- 30 g fine ground cornmeal

What you'll need from the store cupboard:
- 30 g nutritional yeast
- 2 tsps. Cajun seasoning
- 1 tsp. poultry seasoning
- Salt and ground white pepper, to taste

DIRECTIONS
1. Preheat the Air fryer to 195 ºC and grease an Air fryer basket.
2. Mix together cornmeal, nutritional yeast, Cajun seasoning, poultry seasoning, salt and white pepper in a bowl.
3. Coat the soy curls generously with this mixture and arrange in the Air fryer basket.
4. Air fry for about 10 minutes, flipping in between and dis out in a serving platter.

Nutrition Facts Per Serving:
Calories: 317, Fat: 10.2g, Carbohydrates: 30.8g, Sugar: 2g, Protein: 29.4g, Sodium: 145mg

---

Streaky Rasher Filled Poppers

⏱ *PREP TIME: 5 MINUTES, COOK TIME: 15 MINUTES, SERVES 4*

INGREDIENTS
- 4 cooked streaky rashers
- 15 g butter
- 90 g jalapeno peppers, diced
- 65 g almond flour
- 55 g Cheddar cheese, white, shredded

What you'll need from the store cupboard:
- 1 pinch cayenne pepper
- 15 ml streaky rasher fat
- 1 tsp. coarse salt
- Black pepper, ground, to taste

DIRECTIONS
1. Preheat the Air fryer to 200 ºC and grease an Air fryer basket.
2. Mix together butter with salt and water on medium heat in a frying pan.
3. Whisk in the flour and sauté for about 3 minutes.
4. Dish out in a bowl and mix with the remaining ingredients to form a dough.
5. Wrap clingfilm around the dough and refrigerate for about half an hour.
6. Make small popper balls out of this dough and arrange in the Air fryer basket.
7. Air fry for about 15 minutes and dish out to serve warm.

Nutrition Facts Per Serving:
Calories: 385, Fat: 32.8g, Carbohydrates: 5.2g, Sugar: 0.4g, Protein: 17g, Sodium: 1532mg

CHAPTER 8
DESSERT RECIPES

Almond Chocolate Cake / 63

Cream Cheese Cupcakes / 63

Creamy Raspberry Cupcakes / 64

Cream Doughnuts / 64

Chocolate Soufflé / 65

Double Layer Lemon Bars / 65

Lemony Cheesecake / 66

Lemon Mousse / 66

Banana and Walnut Split / 67

Chocolatey Squares / 67

Crème Brûlée / 67

Cinnamon Doughnuts / 68

Chocolate Courgette Brownies / 68

Rustic Almond Tea Biscuits / 68

Lemon Glazed Pop-Tarts / 69

Simple Chocolate Mug Cake / 69

Yoghurt Pecans Chocolate Chip Muffins / 69

Almond Chocolate Cake

⏱ PREP TIME: 10 MINUTES, COOK TIME: 25 MINUTES, SERVES 6

🍸 INGREDIENTS
- 3 eggs
- 100 g almond flour
- 115 g butter, room temperature
- 40 g cocoa powder
- 1½ tsps. baking powder

What you'll need from the store cupboard:
- 115 ml sour cream
- 135 g sugar
- 2 tsps. vanilla

DIRECTIONS
1. Preheat the Air fryer to 180 ºC and grease a cake pan lightly.
2. Mix all the ingredients in a bowl and beat well.
3. Pour the batter in the cake pan and transfer into the Air fryer basket.
4. Bake for about 25 minutes and cut into slices to serve.

Nutrition Facts Per Serving:
Calories: 313, Fat: 134g, Carbohydrates: 5.3g, Sugar: 19g, Protein: 4.6g, Sodium: 62mg

Cream Cheese Cupcakes

⏱ PREP TIME: 10 MINUTES, COOK TIME: 20 MINUTES, SERVES 10

🍸 INGREDIENTS
- 125 g self raising flour
- 15 g cream cheese, softened
- 135 g butter, softened
- 2 eggs
- 35 g fresh raspberries

What you'll need from the store cupboard:
- Pinch of salt
- 120 g caster sugar
- 10 ml fresh lemon juice

DIRECTIONS
1. Preheat the Air fryer to 185 ºC and grease 10 silicon cups.
2. Mix plain flour, baking powder and salt in a bowl.
3. Combine cream cheese, sugar, eggs and butter in another bowl.
4. Mix the flour mixture with the cream cheese mixture and squeeze in the lemon juice.
5. Transfer the mixture into 10 silicon cups and top each cup with 2 raspberries.
6. Place the silicon cups in the Air fryer basket and bake for about 20 minutes.
7. Dish out and serve to enjoy.

Nutrition Facts Per Serving:
Calories: 209, Fat: 12.5g, Carbohydrates: 22.8g, Sugar: 12.4g, Protein: 2.7g, Sodium: 110mg

Creamy Raspberry Cupcakes

⏱ PREP TIME: 15 MINUTES, COOK TIME: 15 MINUTES, SERVES 10

INGREDIENTS
- 125 g self raising flour
- ½ tsp. baking powder
- 15 g cream cheese, softened
- 135 g butter, softened
- 80 g fresh raspberries

What you'll need from the store cupboard:
- A pinch of salt
- 125 g caster sugar
- 10 ml fresh lemon juice

DIRECTIONS
1. Preheat the Air fryer to 160 ºC and grease 10 silicon cups lightly.
2. Mix flour, baking powder, and salt in a large bowl until well combined.
3. Combine well the cream cheese, sugar, eggs, butter, lemon juice and flour mixture in another bowl.
4. Transfer the mixture into silicon cups and place in the Air fryer basket.
5. Bake for about 15 minutes and invert the cupcakes onto wire rack to completely cool.

Nutrition Facts Per Serving:
Calories: 209, Fat: 12.5g, Carbohydrates: 22.8g, Sugar: 12.5g, Protein: 2.7g, Sodium: 110mg

Cream Doughnuts

⏱ PREP TIME: 15 MINUTES, COOK TIME: 16 MINUTES, SERVES 8

INGREDIENTS
- 60 g butter, softened and divided
- 2 egg yolks
- 300 g plain flour
- 1½ tsps. baking powder

What you'll need from the store cupboard:
- 100 g sugar
- 1 tsp. salt
- 115 ml sour cream
- 115 ml double cream

DIRECTIONS
1. Preheat the Air fryer to 180 ºC and grease an Air fryer basket lightly.
2. Sift together flour, baking powder and salt in a large bowl.
3. Add sugar and cold butter and mix until a coarse crumb is formed.
4. Stir in the egg yolks, ½ of the sour cream and 1/3 of the flour mixture and mix until a dough is formed.
5. Add remaining sour cream and 1/3 of the flour mixture and mix until well combined.
6. Stir in the remaining flour mixture and combine well.
7. Roll the dough into 1-cm thickness onto a floured surface and cut into doughnuts with a donut cutter.
8. Coat butter on both sides of the doughnuts and arrange in the Air fryer basket.
9. Bake for about 8 minutes until golden and top with double cream to serve.

Nutrition Facts Per Serving:
Calories: 297, Fat: 13g, Carbohydrates: 40.7g, Sugar: 12.6g, Protein: 5g, Sodium: 346mg

Chapter 8: Dessert Recipes

Chocolate Soufflé

⏱ PREP TIME: 15 MINUTES, COOK TIME: 16 MINUTES, SERVES 2

🏆 INGREDIENTS
- 85 g milk chocolate, chopped
- 60 g butter
- 2 eggs, egg yolks and whites separated
- 15 g plain flour

What you'll need from the store cupboard:
- 45 g sugar
- ½ tsp. pure vanilla extract
- 1 tsp. icing sugar plus extra for dusting

DIRECTIONS
1. Preheat the Air fryer to 165 °C and grease 2 ramekins lightly.
2. Microwave butter and chocolate on high heat for about 2 minutes until smooth.
3. Whisk the egg yolks, sugar, and vanilla extract in a bowl.
4. Add the chocolate mixture and flour and mix until well combined.
5. Whisk the egg whites in another bowl until soft peaks form and fold into the chocolate mixture.
6. Sprinkle each with a pinch of sugar and transfer the mixture into the ramekins.
7. Arrange the ramekins into the Air fryer basket and bake for about 14 minutes.
8. Dish out and serve sprinkled with the icing sugar to serve.

Nutrition Facts Per Serving:
Calories: 569, Fat: 38.8g, Carbohydrates: 54.1g, Sugar: 42.2g, Protein: 6.9g, Sodium: 225mg

---

Double Layer Lemon Bars

⏱ PREP TIME: 10 MINUTES, COOK TIME: 25 MINUTES, SERVES 6

🏆 INGREDIENTS
For the crust:
- 125 g coconut flour, sifted
- 15 g butter, melted

For the lemon topping:
- 3 eggs
- 2 tsps. coconut flour, sifted

What you'll need from the store cupboard:

For the crust:
- 115 g coconut oil, melted
- A pinch of salt
- Sugar, to taste

For the lemon topping:
- Sugar, to taste
- 2 tsps. lemon zest
- 115 ml fresh lemon juice

DIRECTIONS
1. Preheat the Air fryer to 175 ºC and grease a 15-cm baking pan lightly.
2. Mix butter, sugar, salt, and oil in a bowl until foamy.
3. Stir in the coconut flour and mix until a smooth dough is formed.
4. Place the dough into the baking pan and press it thoroughly.
5. Transfer into the Air fryer and bake for about 8 minutes.
6. Meanwhile, whisk eggs with sugar, lemon zest, coconut flour and lemon juice in a bowl and mix well until smooth.
7. Pour this filling into the air fried crust and place into the Air fryer.
8. Set the Air fryer to 190 ºC and bake for about 23 minutes.
9. Cut into slices and serve.

Nutrition Facts Per Serving:
Calories: 301, Fat: 12.2g, Carbohydrates: 2.5g, Sugar: 1.4g, Protein: 8.8g, Sodium: 276mg

Chapter 8: Dessert Recipes

Lemony Cheesecake

⏲ PREP TIME: 10 MINUTES, COOK TIME: 25 MINUTES, SERVES 8

🍷 INGREDIENTS

- 500 g ricotta cheese
- 3 eggs
- 22 g corn starch

What you'll need from the store cupboard:

- 150 g sugar
- 15 ml fresh lemon juice
- 2 tsps. vanilla extract
- 1 tsp. fresh lemon zest, grated finely

🍳 DIRECTIONS

1. Preheat the Air fryer to 160 ºC and grease a baking dish lightly.
2. Mix all the ingredients in a bowl and transfer the mixture into the baking dish.
3. Place the baking dish in the Air fryer basket and bake for 25 about minutes.
4. Dish out and serve immediately.

Nutrition Facts Per Serving:
Calories: 197, Fat: 6.6g, Carbohydrates: 25.7g, Sugar: 19.2g, Protein: 9.2g, Sodium: 102mg

Lemon Mousse

⏲ PREP TIME: 15 MINUTES, COOK TIME: 10 MINUTES, SERVES 3

🍷 INGREDIENTS

- 60 g cream cheese, softened

What you'll need from the store cupboard:

- ¼ tsp. salt
- 1 tsp. lemon liquid stevia
- 80 ml fresh lemon juice
- 350 ml double cream

🍳 DIRECTIONS

1. Preheat the Air fryer to 175 ºC and grease a large ramekin lightly.
2. Mix all the ingredients in a large bowl until well combined.
3. Pour into the ramekin and transfer into the Air fryer.
4. Bake for about 10 minutes and pour into the serving glasses.
5. Refrigerate to cool for about 3 hours and serve chilled.

Nutrition Facts Per Serving:
Calories: 305, Fat: 31g, Carbohydrates: 2.6g, Sugar: 0.4g, Protein: 5g, Sodium: 279mg

Chapter 8: Dessert Recipes

Banana and Walnut Split

PREP TIME: 10 MINUTES, COOK TIME: 10 MINUTES, SERVES 8

INGREDIENTS
- 120 g panko bread crumbs
- 4 bananas, peeled and halved lengthwise
- 60 g cornflour
- 2 eggs
- 10 g walnuts, chopped

What you'll need from the store cupboard:
- 45 g coconut oil
- 45 g sugar
- ¼ tsp. ground cinnamon

DIRECTIONS
1. Preheat the Air fryer to 135 ºC and grease an Air fryer basket lightly.
2. Heat coconut oil in a frying pan on medium heat and add bread crumbs.
3. Cook for 4 minutes until golden brown and transfer into a bowl.
4. Place the flour in a shallow dish and whisk the eggs in another shallow dish.
5. Coat banana slices evenly with flour and dip in eggs and dredge again in the bread crumbs.
6. Mix the sugar and cinnamon in a small bowl and sprinkle over the banana slices.
7. Arrange the banana slices in the Air fryer basket and air fry for about 10 minutes.
8. Top with walnuts and serve.

Nutrition Facts Per Serving:
Calories: 221, Fat: 18.5g, Carbohydrates: 33.7g, Sugar: 12.7g, Protein: 4.8g, Sodium: 115mg

---

Chocolatey Squares

PREP TIME: 15 MINUTES, COOK TIME: 20 MINUTES, SERVES 4

INGREDIENTS
- 60 g cold butter
- 45 g self raising flour
- 7 ml milk
- 60 g chocolate, chopped

What you'll need from the store cupboard:
- 35 g brown sugar
- 40 g honey

DIRECTIONS
1. Preheat the Air fryer to 160 ºC and grease a tin lightly.
2. Mix butter, brown sugar, flour and honey and beat till smooth.
3. Stir in the chocolate and milk and pour the mixture into a tin.
4. Transfer into the Air fryer basket and bake for about 20 minutes.
5. Dish out and cut into desired squares to serve.

Nutrition Facts Per Serving:
Calories: 322, Fat: 15.9g, Carbohydrates: 42.2g, Sugar: 24.8g, Protein: 3.5g, Sodium: 97mg

---

Crème Brûlée

PREP TIME: 10 MINUTES, COOK TIME: 13 MINUTES, SERVES 8

INGREDIENTS
- 10 egg yolks

What you'll need from the store cupboard:
- 950 ml double cream
- 30 g sugar
- 30 ml vanilla extract

DIRECTIONS
1. Preheat the Air fryer to 190 ºC and grease 8 (170 g) ramekins lightly.
2. Mix all the ingredients in a bowl except sugar until well combined.
3. Divide the mixture evenly in the ramekins and transfer into the Air fryer.
4. Bake for about 13 minutes and remove from the Air fryer.
5. Let it cool slightly and refrigerate for about 3 hours.
6. Sprinkle the creams with sugar and caramelize using a crème brûlée iron. Serve immediately.

Nutrition Facts Per Serving:
Calories: 295, Fat: 27.8g, Carbohydrates: 5.8g, Sugar: 3.6g, Protein: 4.6g, Sodium: 33mg

Cinnamon Doughnuts

PREP TIME: 10 MINUTES, COOK TIME: 12 MINUTES, SERVES 6

INGREDIENTS
- 100 g almond flour
- 1 tsp. baking powder
- 30 ml water
- 60 ml almond milk

What you'll need from the store cupboard:
- 50 g sugar
- ½ tsp. salt
- 15 g coconut oil, melted
- 2 tsps. ground cinnamon

DIRECTIONS
1. Preheat the Air fryer to 180 °C and grease an Air fryer basket.
2. Mix flour, 20 g sugar, salt and baking powder in a bowl.
3. Stir in the coconut oil, water, and almond milk until a smooth dough is formed.
4. Cover this dough and refrigerate for about 1 hour.
5. Mix ground cinnamon with 30 g sugar in another bowl and keep aside.
6. Divide the dough into 12 equal balls and roll each ball in the cinnamon sugar mixture.
7. Transfer 6 balls in the Air fryer basket and bake for about 6 minutes.
8. Repeat with the remaining balls and dish out to serve.

Nutrition Facts Per Serving:
Calories: 166, Fat: 4.9g, Carbohydrates: 9.3g, Sugar: 2.7g, Protein: 2.4g, Sodium: 3mg

---

Chocolate Courgette Brownies

PREP TIME: 5 MINUTES, COOK TIME: 35 MINUTES, SERVES 2

INGREDIENTS
- 225 g butter
- 160 g dark chocolate chips
- 300 g courgette, shredded
- ¼ tsp. bread soda
- 1 egg

What you'll need from the store cupboard:
- 1 tsp. vanilla extract
- 80 ml apple sauce, unsweetened
- 1 tsp. ground cinnamon
- ½ tsp. ground nutmeg

DIRECTIONS
1. Preheat the Air fryer to 175 °C and grease 3 large ramekins.
2. Mix all the ingredients in a large bowl until well combined.
3. Pour evenly into the prepared ramekins and smooth the top surface with the back of spatula.
4. Transfer the ramekin in the Air fryer basket and bake for about 35 minutes.
5. Dish out and cut into slices to serve.

Nutrition Facts Per Serving:
Calories: 195, Fat: 18.4g, Carbohydrates: 8.2g, Sugar: 6.4g, Protein: 1.5g, Sodium: 143mg

---

Rustic Almond Tea Biscuits

PREP TIME: 15 MINUTES, COOK TIME: 25 MINUTES, SERVES 3

INGREDIENTS
- 115 g salted butter, softened
- 200 g almond meal
- 1 organic egg

What you'll need from the store cupboard:
- 1 tsp. ground cinnamon
- 2 tsps. sugar
- 1 tsp. organic vanilla extract

DIRECTIONS
1. Preheat the Air fryer to 190 °C and grease an Air fryer basket.
2. Mix all the ingredients in a bowl until well combined.
3. Make equal sized balls from the mixture and transfer in the Air fryer basket.
4. Bake for about 5 minutes and press down each ball with fork.
5. Bake for about 20 minutes and allow the biscuits cool to serve with tea.

Nutrition Facts Per Serving:
Calories: 291, Fat: 14g, Carbohydrates: 30.3g, Sugar: 2.3g, Protein: 11.9g, Sodium: 266mg

Lemon Glazed Pop-Tarts

PREP TIME: 10 MINUTES, COOK TIME: 1 HOUR, SERVES 6

INGREDIENTS
Pop-tarts:
- 125 g coconut flour
- 100 g almond flour
- 115 ml ice-cold water

What you'll need from the store cupboard:
Pop-tarts:
- ¼ tsp. salt
- 30 g sugar
- 155 g cold coconut oil
- ½ tsp. vanilla extract

Lemon Glaze:
- 135 g icing sugar
- 30 ml lemon juice
- zest of 1 lemon
- 5 g coconut oil, melted
- ¼ tsp. vanilla extract

DIRECTIONS
Pop-tarts:
1. Preheat the Air fryer to 190 ºC and grease an Air fryer basket.
2. Mix all the flours, sugar, and salt in a bowl and stir in the coconut oil.
3. Mix well with a fork until an almond flour mixture is formed.
4. Stir in vanilla and 15 ml of cold water and mix until a firm dough is formed.
5. Cut the dough into two equal pieces and spread in a thin sheet.
6. Cut each sheet into 12 equal sized rectangles and transfer 4 rectangles in the Air fryer basket.
7. Bake for about 10 minutes and repeat with the remaining rectangles.

Lemon Glaze:s
8. Meanwhile, mix all the ingredients for the lemon glaze and pour over the cooked tarts.
9. Top with sprinkles and serve.

Nutrition Facts Per Serving:
Calories: 368, Fat: 6g, Carbohydrates: 2.8g, Sugar: 2.9g, Protein: 7.2g, Sodium: 103mg

---

Simple Chocolate Mug Cake

PREP TIME: 15 MINUTES, COOK TIME: 13 MINUTES, SERVES 1

INGREDIENTS
- 35 g self raising flour
- 10 g cocoa powder
- 45 ml milk

What you'll need from the store cupboard:
- 75 g caster sugar
- 45 g coconut oil

DIRECTIONS
1. Preheat the Air fryer to 200 ºC and grease a large mug lightly.
2. Mix all the ingredients in a shallow mug until well combined.
3. Arrange the mug into the Air fryer basket and bake for about 13 minutes.
4. Dish out and serve warm.

Nutrition Facts Per Serving:
Calories: 729, Fat: 43.3g, Carbohydrates: 88.8g, Sugar: 62.2g, Protein: 5.7g, Sodium: 20mg

---

Yoghurt Pecans Chocolate Chip Muffins

PREP TIME: 15 MINUTES, COOK TIME: 10 MINUTES, SERVES 9

INGREDIENTS
- 200 g plain flour
- 2 tsps. baking powder
- 245 g yoghurt
- 40 g mini chocolate chips
- 30 g pecans, chopped

What you'll need from the store cupboard:
- 50 g sugar
- ½ tsp. salt
- 80 ml rapeseed oil
- 2 tsps. vanilla extract

DIRECTIONS
1. Preheat the Air fryer to 180 ºC and grease 9 muffin moulds lightly.
2. Mix flour, sugar, baking powder, and salt in a bowl.
3. Mix the yoghurt, oil, and vanilla extract in another bowl.
4. Fold in the chocolate chips and pecans and divide the mixture evenly into the muffin moulds.
5. Arrange the muffin moulds into the Air fryer basket and bake for about 10 minutes.
6. Remove the muffin moulds from Air fryer and invert the muffins onto wire rack to cool completely before serving.

Nutrition Facts Per Serving:
Calories: 246, Fat: 12.9g, Carbohydrates: 27.3g, Sugar: 10.2g, Protein: 5g, Sodium: 159mg

APPENDIX 1:
MEASUREMENT CONVERSION CHART

WEIGHT EQUIVALENTS

METRIC	US STANDARD	US STANDARD (OUNCES)
15 g	1 tablespoon	1/2 ounce
30 g	1/8 cup	1 ounce
60 g	1/4 cup	2 ounces
115 g	1/2 cup	4 ounces
170 g	3/4 cup	6 ounces
225 g	1 cup	8 ounces
450 g	2 cups	16 ounces
900 g	4 cups	2 pounds

VOLUME EQUIVALENTS

METRIC	US STANDARD	US STANDARD (OUNCES)
15 ml	1 tablespoon	1/2 fl.oz.
30 ml	2 tablespoons	1 fl.oz.
60 ml	1/4 cup	2 fl.oz.
125 ml	1/2 cup	4 fl.oz.
180 ml	3/4 cup	6 fl.oz.
250 ml	1 cup	8 fl.oz.
500 ml	2 cups	16 fl.oz.
1000 ml	4 cups	1 quart

TEMPERATURES EQUIVALENTS

CELSIUS (C)	FAHRENHEIT (F) (APPROXIMATE)
120 °C	250 °F
135 °C	275 °F
150 °C	300 °F
160 °C	325 °F
175 °C	350 °F
190 °C	375 °F
205 °C	400 °F
220 °C	425 °F
230 °C	450 °F
245°C	475 °F
260 °C	500 °F

LENGTH EQUIVALENTS

METRIC	IMPERIAL
3 mm	1/8 inch
6 mm	1/4 inch
1 cm	1/2 inch
2.5 cm	1 inch
3 cm	1 1/4 inches
5 cm	2 inches
10 cm	4 inches
15 cm	6 inches
20 cm	8 inches

APPENDIX 2: RECIPES INDEX

A
Asparagus
Asparagus with Almond / 18
Aubergine
Curried Aubergine / 19
Avocado
Crispy Avocado Chips / 56

B
Baby Bella Mushroom
Egg Mushroom Frittata / 12
Banana
Banana and Walnut Split / 67
Beef
Beef and Veggie Spring Rolls / 50
Mustard Cheesy Beef Meatballs / 52
Beef Flank Steak
Veggie Stuffed Beef Rolls with Pesto / 53
Beef Stewing Steak
Authentic Beef Pot Pie / 50
Breakfast Sausage
Cheddar Breakfast Pockets / 16
Broccoli
Cheese Broccoli Quiche / 10
Broccoli and Cauliflower / 19
Spicy Chilli Broccoli Poppers / 58
Butternut Squash
Cumin Butternut Squash / 20
Stuffed Butternut Squash / 24

C
Carrot
Aromatic Carrots / 18
Catfish
Southern Style Catfish with Mustard / 43
Cauliflower
Hot Cauliflower Poppers / 57
Chicken
Chicken and Broccoli Quiche / 11
Curried Chicken and Onion / 28
Chicken Breast
Cheesy Spinach Stuffed Chicken Breasts / 27
Chicken with Artichoke Hearts / 31
Chicken Breasts with Chimichurri / 33
Crispy Chicken Tenders / 32   *NO*
Streaky Rasher Wrapped Chicken Breasts / 30
Chicken Sausage
Spicy Sausage Streaky Rasher Fandango / 13
Chicken Tender
Sweet and Sour Chicken Kabobs / 35
Chicken Thigh
Chicken and Pepper Kabobs / 28
Jerk Chicken, Pineapple and Veggie Kabobs / 34
Fried Almond Chicken Thighs / 29
Chicken Wing
Sweet Chicken Wings / 30
BBQ Chicken Wings / 27
Chocolate
Chocolate Soufflé / 65
Chocolatey Squares / 67
Chocolate Chip
Yoghurt Pecans Chocolate Chip Muffins / 69
Chorizo Sausage
Feta Sausage Frittata / 12
Courgette
Cheesy Courgette Fritters / 10
Breakfast Courgette and Pepper / 9
Chocolate Courgette Brownies / 68
Crab
Buttered Crab Shells / 38
Rice in Crab Shell / 42
Wasabi Crab and Celery Cakes / 44

D, F-H
Duck Breast
Beer Coated Duck Breast and Cherry Tomatoes / 31
Duck Leg
Five-Spice Duck Legs / 33
Flounder
Breaded Flounder with Lemon / 41
Grape Tomato
Eggs, Tomato and Mushrooms Scramble / 15
Haddock
Sesame Seeds Coated Haddock / 44
Hake
Breaded Hake Fillets / 37
Halibut
Crispy Panko Halibut Strips / 41
Ham
Toad-in-the-Hole Tarts / 13

Cheesy Ham Rolls / 46
Heirloom Tomato
Heirloom Tomato Sandwiches with Pesto / 60

J
Jalapeno Pepper
Streaky Rasher Filled Poppers / 61

L
Lamb
Spicy Lamb Kebabs with Pistachios / 52
Lamb with Potatoes / 52
Lamb Chop
Simple Lamb Chops / 53
Lamb Leg
Roasted Lamb with Rosemary / 49
Lamb Leg with Brussels Sprouts / 51
Lamb Loin Chop
Lemony Lamb Loin Chops / 48
Mustard Lamb Loin Chops / 48
Lamb Sirloin Steak
Spiced Lamb Sirloin Steaks / 49

M,O
Mushroom
Delightful Mushrooms / 21
Cheese Stuffed Mushrooms / 55
Stuffed Mushrooms with Carrot / 61
Okra
Chilli Stuffed Okra / 20
Balsamic Okra with Runner Beans / 22

P
Pak Choi
Cheesy Pak Choi and Egg Frittata / 14
Parsnip
Spicy Honey Parsnips / 21
Pork Belly
Five Spice Pork Belly / 46
Pork Chop
Panko Pork Chops / 51
Garlic Pork Chops / 47
Pork Cutlet
Tomato Stuffed Pork Roll / 53
Potato
Tex-Mex Hash Browns / 16
Hasselback Potatoes / 22
Parmesan Stuffed Potatoes / 23
Prawn
Chilli Panko Prawns / 39
Breaded Prawns with Lemon Zest / 37
Prawn Burgers with Greens / 43
Garlic Lemon Prawns / 40
Crispy Prawns / 57
Pumpkin
Healthy Pumpkin and Tomato Lasagne / 59

R
Radish
Radish Sticks / 60
Raspberry
Creamy Raspberry Cupcakes / 64
Cream Cheese Cupcakes / 63
Red Chilli Pepper
Creamy Chilli Soufflé / 14
Runner Bean
Lemony Runner Beans / 22
Runner Beans and Button Mushroom Bake / 24

S
Salmon
Lemony Coconut Crusted Salmon / 42
Sausage
Sausage Solo / 15
Air Fryer Sausage / 9
Italian Sausage Meatballs / 47
Sea Scallop
Buttered Sea Scallops / 38
Creamy Scallops with Spinach / 41
Sunflower Seed
Fluffy Sunflower Seeds Bread / 59

T
Tofu
Garlic Tofu and Mushroom Omelette / 15
Tofu with Orange Sauce / 25
Peanut Butter Tofu / 23
Tofu with Capers Sauce / 25
Rice Flour Crusted Tofu / 60
Tomato
Cheese Broccoli Stuffed Tomatoes / 59
Tuna
Tuna and Celery Cakes / 40
Creamy Tuna Cakes / 39
Turkey Breast
Easy Turkey Breast / 29
Glazed Turkey Breast / 34
Turkey Leg
Sweet Sriracha Turkey Legs / 35
Turkey Sausage
Breakfast Sausage and Potato Bake / 14
Turkey Wing
Delightful Turkey Wings / 32

Printed in Great Britain
by Amazon